THE POWER TO BECOME

The Power to Become

Wayne McDill

Fleming H. Revell Company
Old Tappan, New Jersey

Library of Congress Cataloging in Publication Data

McDill, Wayne.
    The power to become.

        1. Christian life—1960–   2. Self-actualization.
I. Title.
BV4501.2.M224   248'.4   79-13034
ISBN 0-8007-1053-3

Contents

6   Contents

Preface:
Before We Begin . . .

We had run about two miles and were walking a few more laps to cool down. The discussion had turned to those things most important to a fifteen-year-old with a rather serious Christian outlook on life. We talked about the ups and downs, the times of faithfulness and the dismal failures. We pondered some of the truths of the Christian life most relevant to the complex and very special turmoil of the teen years.

"You ought to write about some of these things," he said. "I think a lot of people don't really understand how to handle all these problems that come with being a Christian."

"You may be right," I responded, as I thought back over some of the things we had been discussing. Maybe these problems really weren't peculiar to the teen years. Maybe Michael had brought them up because we had talked so often before and tried to cope with the weighty but very practical challenges of modern discipleship. Maybe he was just young enough and honest enough to bring right out into the open those very personal struggles the rest of us suffer in quiet frustration.

What about these ideas? Were they new? No, not really. They were basic enough to the teachings of the Bible. But maybe we were trying to get at problems deeper than the surface appearance of things. We had been talking about the Christian life in terms of becoming. We had recounted the vast array of prom-

8 *Preface*

ised resources the Father brings to bear to guarantee our success. We had discussed that grand design of God for all creation and for our lives as individuals.

Then the discussion had become very practical. How can you overcome your own wrong feelings and attitudes? What does God think when you try to be faithful and fail so often? What should you really concentrate on anyway? Is the Christian life a matter of keeping the rules; or is it a matter of acting like a Christian, even if you know inside you're all out of shape? How can I understand myself well enough to know what's going on in my own moods and feelings?

I thought of my own pilgrimage in the Christian life. I had struggled with these same problems. I had been so determined to do for God whatever He wanted. I went from one key to the Christian life, to another. First it was humility, then faith, then love, then discipline. And on I went, like a bee searching for the right flower to solve all my problems.

I remembered that verse, "But as many as received him, to them gave he power to become the sons of God . . ." (John 1:12 KJV). We are children of the heavenly Father, all right. But our becoming has only begun. What a promise, though! He has given us *the power to become.* As our birthright, He has promised us everything we need for the fulfillment of His purpose for us.

So out of that very open discussion in the cool of one early evening came the decision to write some of these things down. In the chapters that follow, I will attempt to get to the heart of some of those struggles in our becoming. Some of the ideas may seem new, even revolutionary. But they are not. And yet, in a sense, they must be new in every generation, if we are to trust the Father for all He has included in the power to become.

1

Becoming Who You Are

"I'm free years old an' I'm bi–ig!" he said as he stretched upward to his full height of thirty-six inches. He was already expressing that natural desire to grow, to become what he was intended to be. I was reminded of how my mother used to have my brother and me stand against the wall to measure our heights. She would carefully mark how tall each of us was and date that mark. We were always proud of the progress we made.

There was built into us a desire to grow, to make progress, to attain our full potential. I guess I never got over that. Through my teen years and as an adult, I have felt the urge to be growing, developing, becoming. Maybe this is a part of what it means to be alive. It seems that all nature has this inner drive to grow, to reach onward and upward, to develop to its fullest potential.

Who could imagine a baby chick not working to peck its way out of its egg and get on with the business of becoming a chicken? Who can imagine a newborn colt not giving his full attention to those awkward attempts to get to his feet? He somehow knows he has important business—becoming a horse. Who can imagine a caterpillar being confused about spinning that cocoon and getting on with becoming a butterfly? The seeds of becoming are built into nature's every expression of life.

With man, however, there seems to be some confusion. As a child, every boy knows he is to become a man. We teach him that much. But somehow all he knows about being a man is that a man is bigger. So his great goal is to "get big." Our four-year-old and I were having one of those look-how-big-you're-getting conversations the other day. So I asked him how he managed to be getting bigger and bigger. "Milk and birthdays," he answered. Drinking enough milk and having enough birthdays will take you a long way, but we suspect that there's more to it than that.

If we have them at birth, our instincts as to what we're really supposed to become somehow get lost along the way. We are not programmed with the right automatic responses. With our power of reason and our freedom of choice, the possibilities open to us seem almost limitless. In fact, there are so many ways to aim our lives that it is easy to miss our real reason for being.

After we begin to "get big," we tend to lose our sense of direction. Our vision of the adventure of becoming fades into confusion. Even in the teen years, a vast majority of young people have no idea what they will do with their lives. This same uncertainty follows many to college and beyond. All they can do is follow the example of others around them, who often won't admit that they don't know where they are going, either.

Finding the Real You

"Will the real Norman Finklewartz please stand up?" The tension continues to mount as the audience waits to see who is the real person and who are the imposters. The panel has interviewed all four men in an effort to determine which of the four is the one they all claim to be. The interview period comes to a close, and each panelist votes for his choice. Only then does the real Norman Finklewartz stand up.

A beginning point for knowing who you are to become may well be finding the real you. We might say, "Will the real you please stand up?" Just as on the TV game show, there might be some hesitation and uncertainty. Many of us are no more sure about who we are than we are about what we should be doing with our lives. Oh, we can give you names, addresses, and other facts and figures like that. But, beyond those surface items, we're stumped.

If you were asked to tell who you are, without using any names, addresses, numbers, or physical descriptions, what would you say? Maybe you would use relationships: "I am the one who is my husband's wife." Perhaps you would say you are the person who did this or that and refer to your past accomplishments. What about professions: carpenter, draftsman, student, homemaker? Or maybe you could talk about race, nationality, where you grew up, political party, or church affiliation.

In every case, though, it seems an indignity to reduce the whole of your unique being to a label and stuff all you are into that limited category. In fact, it just won't work. When we label someone—Democrat, vegetarian, Presbyterian, Italian—we reduce him to something small enough to be slipped neatly into a pigeonhole. This is like making a cartoon caricature of yourself. It's not you. You are far too complex for that.

Everyone you have met and every experience you have had has contributed something, however small, to who you are. Whether you think of yourself as the victim or the beneficiary of your background, you are nevertheless shaped by it. Though the name you received at birth may have had little meaning at the time, you have since invested it with meaning for those who know you. It stands for you. The mention of your name brings to another's mind a flood of ideas and impressions he has received from you.

As human beings, we are somehow discontent with being only the sum total of the influences which have shaped us. We want to think our significance as individuals reaches beyond the limitations of our experience. After all, we can ask such questions as: Who am I? Why am I here? Where am I going? and What is my purpose in life? The very fact that we wonder about such things seems to point to meaning for our lives that reaches far beyond us.

The Clue to Character

That question, "Who am I?" seems to be the big one. Here I am, walking around in this body, looking out at all those other "whos," having thoughts in here that they can't hear, being alone in here. I sense I am somehow unique, somehow special. Is who I am already determined? Do I have no choice in the matter, or do I awaken someday to realize that up to this point much unused potential has been given, and now t's up to me to do something with it?

The best clue to who you really are may be found in a look at your priorities. What is really important to you? What is that thing for which you are willing to sacrifice almost everything else? Unfortunately, some groping wanderers among us might say that survival is their highest priority. But having survival as the chief aim is a matter for sick people. Those who are healthy will be up and at the business of living.

What you value most will clearly reflect who you are now and who you are becoming. Is it pleasure? Will you make sacrifices and decide important matters in terms of the pleasure it will bring you? What about prestige and approval by others? Does your whole life revolve around what others think and how to gain their approval and admiration? How about possessions? Do you devote most of your thought, time, and energy to making money?

The answers to these questions tell much more about you than your name, address, or any label we could attach to you. Not only do your priorities tell who you are now, they also forecast who you will become. You will inevitably become like that which you value most. Your very character and attitude are shaped by whatever you set as your goals in life, even if you are not consciously aware of these aims.

We tend to confuse means and ends. We look around us at people who appear to be successful in life. They are striving to achieve, earn, attain, and accomplish. So we conclude that this is what life is all about. This must be our reason for being. But is that all there was in the potential of that marvelous, tiny new creature you once were? Or was there, in your being, the seed of becoming that goes far beyond the value of any temporary accomplishments?

What if we look at nature in the same way? What if we conclude that the reason a caterpillar exists is to build cocoons? We could go on to say that a bird's reason for being is to build nests, a beaver's for building dams, and a salmon's for swimming upstream against the raging current. These are laudable accomplishments. We are fascinated with the beauty and complexity of these feats of engineering and endurance.

These marvelous deeds are, however, only means to the end given to each of these creatures. The final goal in each case has to do with coming to maturity and preserving the species. Building cocoons and nests and dams are merely appropriate tasks along the way. What if a caterpillar only built a cocoon, then a larger one, then a nicer one, then a four-bedroom model with a double garage? What if he were so busy building cocoons, that he forgot to become a butterfly? He would be a failure in his one great purpose for being.

Within each of us there is that hunger to become all we were intended to be. We often don't even recognize it. We sense the restlessness, but fail to realize that we will never really be satisfied with life until we know why we are here and get about that purpose. We may try to fill our emptiness by building dams and nests, or by swimming upstream toward some superhuman achievement. We call that thing we're looking for "happiness," not knowing that real happiness is only found on the way to becoming the person we were created to be.

It's so easy to fall into the pattern in vogue around us. Just like everybody else, we chase after those elusive symbols of success and happiness: fame, fun, and fortune. But somehow we know there must be more to life than this. The idea occasionally brushes our thoughts that there is some grand design so intricate and complex that it is beyond our comprehension. Somehow, in those quiet moments, you know that even you have a place in that cosmic scheme.

Why Am I Here?

When we talk about *becoming* for humankind we are getting into the question of the purpose, the meaning, the intention that is implied in our very existence. We are here. That seems sure enough. Why we're here is another question. This requires us to go back and ask, "Who put me here?" But some modern thinkers would answer, "Nobody put you here. You are the result of a long series of benign mutations which have accidentally occurred over the span of millions of years of evolution."

If that's true, there is no meaning for my life. I'm only an accident of the impersonal Nature of which I'm a part. There's no use even discussing who I am supposed to become. I don't have anything to say about it. It's all determined by Nature. I act out my little drama, according to forces within and around me that I cannot affect in any way. All my choices are already programmed by Nature.

In this deterministic view, I have no more purpose for being than any other form of life. My lofty ideas about character, free choice, dreams, meaning, goals, and greatness are all no more significant than the baby chick pecking its way out of its egg. The only meaning for my life is confined to the natural processes which make up this closed system. Nature is all there is, and I'm only a part of Nature. Man is alone in the universe as a thinking being.

But somehow it's hard to believe there isn't Somebody out there beyond the system, who put it all together. In fact, it takes more faith to believe all the universe is an accident than to believe God made it all on purpose. After considering only a small part of the evidence, I've decided to believe there is Somebody outside Nature. I believe He made it, that He made it on purpose, that He is still operating it, and that He had something in mind when He made me.

Since I believe I'm here on purpose, I am very interested in knowing what that purpose is. I only have one turn at life, so it seems best to get it right the first time. Several options are open to me:

- I can ignore the idea of purpose and concentrate on some kind of pleasant survival.
- I can try to come up with a life purpose on my own, without reference to any meaning from beyond.
- I can try to understand the purpose of the One who created me in the first place.

Knowing the Designer

A good beginning point for understanding something about that grand design is to learn something about the Designer. What kind of Person is it who made all that is, and did it on purpose? Well, for one thing, He is a Person, and not Nature itself or some impersonal force. He is a reasoning, intelligent Designer. No one can examine the amazing consistency, functionality, and beauty of creation without being impressed. This is no accident.

If the Creator is personal, what is His name? Moses asked the One who spoke to him out of the burning bush about His name. He answered, ". . . I am who I am . . . . This is my name forever . . ." (Exodus 3:14, 15). So God said that His name should be called I AM. He is the One who was and is and ever shall be. He is perfect being and person. Jesus of Nazareth was closely questioned by the religious leaders of His day. They also asked who He was. He answered, ". . . I Am Who I Am" (John 8:24, 28).

Becoming is the key to our growth, because God, the I AM, is at work to bring creation into consistency with His own character. This character was demonstrated in Jesus Christ in such a way that we can understand it. It is His desire that we ". . . become mature people, reaching to the very height of Christ's full stature" (Ephesians 4:13). So our becoming is to be in terms of character and spirit, as we see them in Jesus Christ.

It is natural for us to see the kind of life God requires as a matter of doing. The Bible seems to be full of instructions and commands. So, many a Christian sets out to do something for God that will impress Him with the believer's earnestness. This idea brings to the religious dimension the same efforts men apply to life in general. They are ever accomplishing, attaining, collecting, experiencing, knowing. It seems right, then, to try to do these things to please and impress God.

But God is the I AM, who desires to bring our character and spirit into consistency with His own. Being comes before doing. Your doing is only meaningful as it reflects your becoming. In light of the Creator's infinite wealth, what can you possibly give Him that He needs? In light of His infinite power, what can you possibly do for Him that He cannot accomplish without you? Actually, the whole religious idea of impressing God with our doing and giving is contrary to New Testament truth.

Character, Not Accomplishment

God's concern for man is moral character. He is much more interested in close personal fellowship with us than He is in any favors we might attempt to do for Him. Jesus, His own Son, did not come to show us how to *do* things for God. He came to demonstrate in His life complete harmony with the *purpose* of the Father. His magnificent obsession was to please the Father. He wanted only to perfectly fulfill that divine intention for His life.

Notice what Jesus said in the Sermon on the Mount. This statement is often misunderstood. He said, "You must be perfect—just as your Father in heaven is perfect" (Matthew 5:48). We interpret that word *perfect* to mean "flawless." We think God wants us to concentrate on being 100 percent error free. But the word translated *perfect* really has to do with purpose. Our goal is not to strive for flawlessness, but to stay in step with our Creator's intentions for us.

God's intention, as the I AM, is to bring all creation into perfect harmony with His own character and purpose. This means He is much more interested in our becoming than in our doing. Behavior comes naturally from the kind of person you are. Behavior reveals what is within, in character and spirit. So if we will concentrate on becoming like the I AM, as we know Him in Jesus Christ, our behavior will follow suit.

All the instructions and commands of the Bible are a "therefore" ethic. Man is never commanded to behave in order to make it with God. He is only commanded to behave because of the *therefore* of God's purpose and power. God never requires anything of us for which He does not provide all the resources necessary for obedience. "I have promised you the power and guidance, *therefore* obey Me," He says. All His instructions are based on who you are in His purpose and what He is doing to make you able.

A Model for Becoming

God provides quite a picture of the person He has in mind for you to become. The Bible describes you as alert to the wishes of the Father and determined to please Him. You are free, within the bounds of His grand design, to be master of yourself and your life, because you are shaping it according to His plan. You know the joy of being in step with the beat of all creation. You can embrace life to its fullest. You can be positive, sensitive, and caring toward others because all of this is part of the character He is building in you.

Each of us has in his mind a picture of the person he'd like to be. This ideal self is a combination of qualities we like in others and the desire to overcome our own frustrating weaknesses. We look at the particular strengths of others and wish to be like them. "He's so cool and collected—always has everything under control." "She's so gracious, so sensitive to others." "I wish I could be outgoing and confident like him."

Though our own weaknesses and the good qualities we see in others give us an idea of the person we'd like to be, our model for becoming is Jesus Christ. In character and spirit, in attitude and behavior, He always demonstrated God's idea of what a man should be. The Bible makes clear that the purpose of the I AM is to work in your own life to form the very character of Christ in you.

The Bible says that God has set every Christian apart to be like His Son. He works in every circumstance for the accomplishment of this purpose. He refuses to give up on you, working not only to give you a desire for the character of Christ, but also empowering you for that aim. We read that those who received Christ were given the power to become children of God.

This world then becomes a training ground for Christ-like character. The tensions, stresses, and challenges of life only serve to strengthen those qualities God is developing in us. A physician told a friend of mind to avoid any situation that might cause her stress or tension. I couldn't help but wonder where she might go in this world to find such an environment. But for the person who is trusting in God and His purpose, these tests only provide exercise for his spiritual muscles.

The Real Picture

Maybe you're saying to yourself, "That sure doesn't sound like me." Well, it may take a little time to get used to this picture of yourself. This is you in light of your reason for being, in light of God's intention when He made you. This picture is based on what He does for you and in you that you could never do on your own. It is not based on who you are without God, but who you are only because you are His.

"But wait a minute," you say. "If I don't feel like what you've described, and other people don't see me that way, then is God's description of me just make-believe?" No! God's picture of you is not make-believe; it's the real you. Your picture of yourself and the image others have of you will not last. That picture will change. But the picture God has of you is the real you, the person everyone will one day recognize you to be.

It's like this. With God, the person He describes you to be is *already*. With you, this picture of yourself is *not yet*. So you are to become who you are. Because what God says is obviously *not yet* to you, it is easy to get confused and think God's picture is *not at all*. But don't ever be mistaken about it; God is not finished with you yet. He plans to change who you are *not yet* into who He knows you to be *already*. The distance between the two is your "becoming gap."

Thinking It Through

• Everyone wants to be somebody. No one wants to be nobody. Your Creator, the I AM, made you in the first place to be somebody very special. He made you to be of the same character as His Son, Jesus Christ. The heavenly Father already sees you with all those qualities, and challenges you to become who you are in Christ. He is at work in your life right now to accomplish that purpose.

• Stop and think about your goals for yourself. Now,

what about your aims for your children, husband, or wife? Do you strive to make your children happy or to guide them in becoming Christlike in character? If you prepare them to make a living or gain prominence or enjoy life, could they still miss their reason for being? If, on the other hand, you aim at building character, will they not be more likely to have the moral fiber to become successful and fulfilled in these other areas?

• How do you respond to stress and trouble in your world? Do you see these negative circumstances as enemies, or do you see them as part of the training exercises in character building which the Father is pleased to lead you through? How you respond to life's thorns and scrapes may not tell others much about your situation, but it can tell them a lot about you.

• Our challenge of becoming calls for special understanding at several crucial points. I will try to clear up some misconceptions in several of these areas in the chapters to follow. How do you get a right start for becoming? How does your self-image need to be changed? How can you live by faith? How do you resolve your inner struggles? How can beliefs and behavior be consistent? How can you know God's attitude toward you? How can you have the power to live this becoming adventure?

2
Beginning at the Right Place

At the summer Olympics in 1976, a new feature was introduced to insure that everyone got off to an equal start in the races. The starting blocks for those races were wired to electronic equipment which could sense whether any runner left the block before the starting gun sounded. If someone jumped the gun, a loud warning would go off, indicating a false start. The race would have to begin again. A sophisticated means of measurement is customary at the finish of a race, but a proper start is also necessary if each runner is to accomplish all his skills and strength will allow.

A right start is vital. But there are so many ways to make a wrong start. You may remember the incident at the Olympics in Germany several years ago, when some of the American athletes received a faulty schedule. Some of them were late for their track-and-field events, and so were disqualified. Others showed up at the wrong place for their races and missed the events they were supposed to run. In the challenge of becoming who you are, a right start is also vital. It's easy to start the wrong way, at the wrong place, in the wrong race, or with a false start.

The Search for a New Start

There's not one of us who hasn't wished at some time or another for a chance to start all over. We'd like to begin again and leave all the mistakes and failures of the past behind. We'd like to forget those things which bring the dark feelings of guilt and remorse. How good it would be to start with a clean slate and new possibilities, with no list of fouls already chalked up against us.

One young husband was impressed with a beautiful fresh-baked pie when he arrived home from work. His bride glowed with pride as he remarked about the golden brown crust. He didn't say anything, however, about the several not-quite-right pie crusts he later noticed in the garbage container. The young wife had kept on starting over till she got it right. Like her, most of us leave quite a trail of not-quite-right attempts at success.

We are encouraged by the saying, "Today is the first day of the rest of your life." We feel a fresh swell of hope that we can start all over today to do better than we've done in the past. So we try to contrive new beginnings and talk ourselves into thinking they are real. We make New Year's Resolutions and hope that somehow January first will bring a new start. We take new jobs, move to new towns, build new houses, get new hairdos, and make ourselves all kinds of promises that things are going to be different from now on.

Somehow, though, by the second or third week in

January we find out that the new year is not really new at all. Sometimes a new job, a new town, a new house may help. But we usually find that we move into these new relationships, dragging all the annoying problems we had before, just like tin cans after a wedding car.

So I've come to the conclusion that what really needs to be changed is not the circumstances and situations. What is needed is a new me. No matter what the circumstances that gang around me, it's who I am within myself that determines how those problems and situations will be interpreted. Will I see them as enemies that threaten my well-being, or will I see them as problem-solving opportunities to challenge my creativity and get the old juices flowing?

Natural Man

I am never surprised when my dog acts doggish. It just comes natural to him to be dogly about everything. In fact, I am sure it never occurred to Spot ever to be anything but doglike. That's his nature. There's built into his system of instincts and intelligence a computer program entitled "dog." He comes into this world with built-in tail-wagging, panting, ball-chasing, and hand-licking activities already on his schedule.

Let's notice one other thing about Spot, while we've got him on our counseling couch. Notice that he did not become a dog by acting like one. That's very important. Sometimes we think you can become a new person by acting like one. But that won't work.

I suppose it's possible for old Spot to go berserk and try to become a cat. He could meow like a cat, eat cat food, rub up against your leg, and do all those other catty things, but he would still be old Spot. In fact, if he started acting like that, he might not retain the privilege of being old Spot much longer. Sometimes people may do that: try so hard to be somebody they are not that they wind up being nobody at all.

Let's come back then to you and me and ask the question I really have in mind. What is our nature as human beings? Without aiming for a complete list, think about several things that are natural to human nature.

- Man is gregarious, bunching up in groups: families, villages, cities, and nations.
- Man is territorial: He likes to mark off some space in life to call his own and protect that space from any intruders.
- Man is creative: He likes to rearrange some of his environment in such a way as to express his own sense of beauty.
- Man is rational: He can think, even about himself, and visualize ideas and decisions in abstract form in his mind.
- Man is a conqueror, ever climbing mountains, exploring the unknown, overcoming disease, and generally trying to take charge of his world.
- Man is a communicator, sharing everything from the subtlest nuances of thought to the most practical descriptions of fact.

And on and on we could go, describing man—the pinnacle and masterpiece of God's creative activity. But let's look at man from a different viewpoint. Let's consider man from the perspective of God's purpose. How does man's nature affect the things God has in mind? Why does God's picture of you and me sometimes sound so foreign to the normal experience of man?

How a Good Idea Went Sour

God made people, in the first place, because He thought it was a good idea. In making them, He created them with a nature perfectly compatible with the fulfillment of all His plans for them. Things were going great. But then tragedy struck. In order for their relationship with Him to be based on trust and obedience rather than coercion and repression, God had given men the freedom either to accept or reject His divine authority.

Accepting God's authority meant giving God the freedom He has built into that relationship. Giving God that freedom would mean that God would be in charge of setting the priorities, determining the standards, and developing the plans for man's life. With that freedom comes the responsibility for providing the resources and guaranteeing the success of the venture.

Rejecting God's authority would mean that man kept the freedom for himself. He would be the one who determined the priorities, established the standards, and developed the plans for his own life. And he would be the one responsible for providing the resources and guaranteeing the success of those plans.

But there was more involved here than deciding who gets the bigger chunk of the freedom. There is also the question of who has a right to rule. Does God have a right to be in authority over man because He is the Creator and because the whole arrangement was His idea in the first place? Or does man have the right to be his own authority because the freedom is there to say yes or no to God's rule? The Genesis story shows us that man decided to take charge himself, grab what looked good, eat what tasted good, and try to get wisdom enough to run his own affairs.

So man took himself out from under God's rule and resources. As a result, God shut the door to keep him out—not because His feelings were hurt, but because this turn of events was more than just an incident of insubordination. In deciding to take over the freedoms and responsibilities that were rightfully God's, man actually put himself in the place of God in his own life.

In becoming lord of his own life, man became an enemy of God, because there can be only one ruler in each kingdom. It was a matter of real rebellion, a matter of setting up a rival system of authority. This attitude of pride and self-sufficiency in man was an offense aimed directly at the Person of God and His purpose for man. God could not tolerate such a condition.

In using the freedom God gave him to choose to be free from God Himself, man made a choice that brought about an ugly change at the center of his being. A major shift took place in the very nature of man. Instead of being focused on the God who made him, his life became focused on himself.

- Rather than seeking God's purposes, he sought his own.
- Rather than worshiping at the altar of God, he set up a new altar in his own heart.

- Rather than learning God's truth and wisdom, he began to develop his own ideas.
- Rather than trusting God for his needs, he began to work out things for himself.
- Rather than trying to please God, he sought to satisfy his own self-centered desires.

From the viewpoint of God's grand design for man, man's nature had gone sour, corrupted to the core. And God called this corruption *sin.* The traits characteristic of man's fallen nature not only erected barriers between himself and God; his relationship with his fellowman was also marked primarily by self-interest and conflict. Just as God had become his enemy as a rival for lordship, so other men became his enemies as rivals for possession of the things man wanted for himself.

God's Plan for a New Start

God was not willing to give up on His grand design. In fact, He had already known that this rebellion of man was always possible with the freedom He had given him. But knowing that, God still thought it far better to give man freedom to choose than to have him obey because he had no choice. After all, what kind of relationship could be built on coercion? No, God wanted their relationship to be built on love.

God's plan to restore man to himself would have to meet several important qualifications.

This plan would have to rightly re-establish God's authority.

It would need to re-establish man's God-given freedom.

The plan would need to effectively remove the sin barrier which separated them.

It would need to recreate man in his inner nature.

Even though men have tried through the ages to accomplish all this with their man-made religion, nothing man can do will restore him to God. The answer had to come from God.

So God took action. He sent His own Son to the earth to demonstrate His love by becoming a man and gathering to Himself all the penalty due for man's sin. He took love where nothing else would go. "But God has shown us how much he loves us—it was while we were still sinners that Christ died for us!" (Romans 5:8).

In His death and resurrection, Jesus Christ effectively re-established God's authority, even over sin, death, and hell. He restored man's real freedom to accept or reject God's authority. He removed the sin barrier by accepting all the penalty of sin Himself on the Cross. He made possible a new selfhood for man, at the center of his being, by taking the old nature to the grave and introducing a new nature in the Resurrection.

God's plan for straightening things out between mankind and Himself actually operated in two worlds. One world is the heavenly world. This is the dimension of reality that is beyond us. We can't see it or touch it or move it. This is where God makes adjustments in His own bookkeeping when someone is restored to Him through Jesus Christ. According to the Bible, the believer's name is then written in the Book of Life. He is put down as acceptable to God through Christ, in spite of his own poor performance. He is acceptable to God because he believes what God has said and what Jesus Christ has done to make it possible for him to be a child of God.

The other dimension of reality is the earthly dimension. In this world there are also some things which take place when a person is restored to God through Jesus Christ. His sense of guilt is removed as his sins are forgiven. He has a new peace in his heart. He has a new ability to hear God's voice and understand His Word. He has new freedom to be the new person God is making him. All this comes with what the Bible calls being born again.

Beginning at the Beginning

To really get a new start, you have to go back to the very beginning. There, at the beginning of your life, you were a squirming, squalling newcomer to the adventure of living. You were a new life, by nature the offspring of your mother and father. You got a lot from them: physical characteristics, temperament, emotional makeup, intellectual abilities, even certain likes and dislikes. All that was a part of your natural beginning.

A new birth is the way Jesus described what happens in a person's life when he comes to God through Christ. Being born again means a completely new start spiritually. You are born anew within by the life-giving power of the Spirit of God. As a newborn member of the family of God, you have a new nature. The corrupted nature you receive at birth is joined by a new nature like the character of Jesus Christ. This sets up the struggle within you for the power to become.

When you are born again, there is a real change at the

center of yourself. The Bible says, "When anyone is joined to Christ, he is a new being; the old is gone, the new has come" (2 Corinthians 5:17). Being born again is not just the adoption of a new religion, nor is it merely a matter of assuming a new devotional attitude toward spiritual things.

Being born again means becoming a new person by the power of God. It means having new characteristics, new qualities, a new outlook on life, a new hope for the future, a new power by the Holy Spirit to become the person God has in mind for you. Being born again is the new beginning you've needed all along, because it's the only new start that starts with a new you.

So now we come back to you and me. We are faced with the choice. Will we allow God to complete His grand design for us? This means confessing our sin, surrendering our tainted freedom to Him, and accepting what God has done in Jesus Christ to restore us to Himself. When you do this, you accept God's priorities, His standard, and His plan for your life. With that, God provides the resources and guarantees the success of the project. To reject God's call to restoration means you insist on running things yourself and accept responsibility for providing the resources and guaranteeing the success of your life.

But remember this: God is looking at things from the viewpoint of forever. Are you? How long can you run things successfully? Is your plan anything like God's grand design? When you finish this one life of yours, will you be pleased with the story? And beyond that, if you choose to live without God now, you will be stuck with that choice when you die. For right now you will also be stuck with the same old you, wishing for things to get better.

Thinking It Through

In this chapter we have been considering the only starting place for the power to become. A right start is vital to your becoming the person God has in mind for you to be in His grand design. Let's get at some practical meaning for these ideas now.

• The key to the power of a new beginning is the kind of beginning it is. New starts related to the calendar or circumstances, or even good intentions, are not adequate. The problem is deeper than that. The change must come from within. It is a change of *who* rather than *what*. Jesus said, "You must be born again." That is the only spiritually dynamic new beginning with permanent results. Be honest with yourself. Have you been born again?

• Here is a prayer. If it expresses your own desire right now, talk with God and surrender your life to Him.

God, I realize how much I need You. Thank You for not giving up on me. I believe that Jesus Christ, Your own Son, died for my sins, to remove the barrier that separates me from You. I want You to have Your way fully in my life. Forgive my sins and make me a new person within. Thank You for Your love and forgiveness. Thank You for accepting me as Your own child through Jesus Christ. Amen.

• Each of us is personally responsible for his own life. The choices we make determine the kind of life that results. We may point to factors we cannot control and blame them for what we experience. But other people, events, and circumstances are not the determining forces in our lives. We are! Just as real change can begin only with me, so can the final responsibility rest only with me. Begin today to refuse shifting blame for undesirable consequences. Practice the policy of boldly accepting responsibility rather than making excuses.

• As a Christian, you have a new freedom to choose the course of your life. But your new freedom is only properly exercised under the rule of God. Think of the choices you have made during the past week. How do they demonstrate your surrender to God's authority? The daily choices you make reflect who you are and determine who you become. Forecast the choices you will be likely to make in the coming week. Plan now how you can choose in such a way as to reflect your new beginning in Christ.

The power to become is the power of a new beginning.

3
Thinking of Yourself in a New Way

She scanned the room with that innocent but detached curiosity babies seem to have, too much of a newcomer to this world to understand very much of what she saw. I held her closer to the mirror, thinking the movement might attract her attention to her reflection in the glass. It worked. Suddenly her eyes locked in on that small, baby-plump figure before her. Her gaze grew brighter and wider as she reached out to touch the little person in the mirror.

As that "other baby" reached forward at the same time for a palm-to-palm greeting through the glass, the revelation seemed to dawn. I'm not sure how babies think. But in whatever form their thoughts take, she was surely saying, *That's me!* Her attentiveness to the fascinated gaze staring back at her through the mirror made it clear. She was being introduced to the one who would soon and forever become one of her favorite people.

What a fascinating thing it is to reflect on the fact that

you are you! This ability to make ourselves the object of
our own thoughts is one of those uniquely human
capacities. Animals can't think about themselves. Oh, I
know, they may scratch their fleas, switch flies, chase
their tails, or groom their fur. But they can't reflect on
their own existence and think about themselves as individual creatures like those they see around them.

When our boys were little, they were quite impressed
when I told them, "Spot doesn't even know there's a dog
named Spot and that he is him." No, Spot may have ob-
served a lot about the children, dogs, cats, and others
around himself, but he never thought much about Spot.
He ate when he was hungry, drank when he was thirsty,
ran when he felt like running, and played when he felt
like playing. But he never sat around meditating on his
unique creaturehood. He never worried about where he
came from, where he was going, and why he was here.

But you and I do think about ourselves. And what we
think of ourselves affects everything we do. You have the
amazing capacity to make yourself the object of your own
thoughts. Now I don't suggest that we sit around cross-
legged, like some mystics I've heard about, and contemplate our own navels. But it is a good exercise to give
some serious thought to who you are. The picture you
have of yourself actually becomes a role you find yourself
playing, without giving it a thought—or even liking it.

Learning to Understand Yourself

"After they made him, they threw away the mold!"
You've probably heard that said of some rather unusual
person. But that's true of us all. When they made you they

threw the mold away. Actually, the mold out of which each one of us was cast was only used one time by our Creator. Every one of us is unique. There's not another person in the entire world just like you or me. And that's not an accident. We're not products of a divine assembly line. Each one of us is a special-order model.

When I was eight or nine, I used to think that with all the billions of people in the world there was surely another little boy, somewhere, just like me. In my daydreams, I imagined that the other little boy probably lived in India or China, somewhere on the other side of the world. I pictured him as being just my age and size and looking just like me. I imagined that if you could translate his name into English, it would turn out to be the same as mine. I even imagined that he might be wondering whether there was a little boy, over on this side of the world, just like him.

In my pilgrimage of thinking about myself, I learned one day that no two snowflakes are just alike. Neither are there any two roses or two cows or two frogs or two mockingbirds which are identical. I could pretty well tell the difference in our cows. (We had them all named.) But frogs and mockingbirds were something else. They all looked alike to me. Anyway, I came to the conclusion that if God used a slightly different pattern for every frog and mockingbird, then surely there were no two people exactly alike, either.

Then I had another problem. Realizing how very unique I was sometimes didn't seem to help very much. If I am actually the only person in the whole earth just like me, then, of all the possibilities of who I might have been, why did I have to be me? After all, I was unusually skinny, had crooked teeth and an extra large nose for a little boy, and endured being called Nose by my thoughtful friends. I could readily understand why God threw the mold away after He made me!

It was always easy to find somebody to compare myself with who had more meat on his bones, a standard-sized nose, and straight teeth. So I fell into a third problem in thinking about myself. I began to compare myself unfavorably with others. I came to the conclusion I was definitely inferior. I was sure others had also come to this conclusion. So I became more and more careful not to put myself in a position that would show me up for the second-rate nobody I was. My philosophy became, "Keep your mouth shut and stay out of sight, and nobody will laugh at you."

Overcoming a Loser's Outlook

I suspect there are a good many others in this world who develop a low opinion of themselves and begin to think there's nothing they can do about it. Every time they seem to fail, they say, "See, that proves it. I just don't have what it takes." And even if they succeed, they don't see any meaning to that. "I was just lucky that time, I guess." We get into the habit of evaluating our own worth on the basis of our performance, but we judge that performance with our minds already made up that we're losers. Whew! What a trap!

One of the greatest problems many of us face is this lack of self-confidence. Inside we are afraid. We shrink back from life because of feelings of inadequacy and insecurity. We are uncertain about our own ability to take hold of our world and make it respond to our own dreams and goals. We are afraid that somehow we just don't have what it takes to become what we really want to be. So we decide just to drift along, accepting less than our own best, giving up on our dreams. We timidly feel our way through life, in the fear that around every corner waits some failure or disaster.

Unfortunately we tend to bring this loser's outlook to the challenge of living the Christian life. We make the same mistakes all over again and wind up defeated, discouraged, disappointed Christians. We compare ourselves with all the apparently successful believers around us and come to the conclusion we've done it again. We've proved ourselves incapable of really coming out on top.

God knows we want to be confident and positive toward life. He made each one of us with a deep desire to be worthy, to count for something, to distinguish himself as special in some way. Jesus said He came to give just that kind of overflowing, positive life. So we can be assured that this is the kind of life God has in mind for us. In fact, God wants to pick us up out of the rut of self-pity, guilt, frustration, and discouragement. He wants to set each of us on the path to becoming a new person.

Shifting the Center of the Universe

How you think about yourself—your self-concept or self-image—affects everything about you. Our natural habit of focusing on ourselves needs to be redirected when we become Christians. We don't stop thinking about ourselves. Our responsibility for what we do with life requires giving attention to what's going on here. But the way we think about ourselves changes. The center of focus changes, and the believer begins to see that the world really does not revolve around him.

The outlook of small children gives us a vivid picture of this human tendency. They see the whole world from the viewpoint of their own desires. Their own wants are the foremost matter of importance. All else is of little consequence. Psychologist Henry Brandt says the first word most children learn is *s'mine*. As we grow up, we learn adult versions of that same self-centered outlook. We become more subtle about it, and even reinterpret our demands in such a way as to make them sound unselfish. Take, for example, the man who spent all his time making money so his "family could have everything they needed."

When a person becomes a Christian, though, the center of his world shifts from self to Christ. This takes some getting used to. It's just not natural to want to give up being the center of the universe. But Jesus said, ". . . If anyone wants to come with me . . . he must forget himself, carry his cross, and follow me. For whoever wants to save his own life will lose it; but whoever loses his life for me and for the gospel will save it" (Mark 8:34, 35). So the only way to find the kind of life you want is to give up your life to make Him your life.

It is natural for us to see our whole world as centered in ourselves. So we bring this focus to our efforts to live the Christian life. We see the drama of discipleship centered in ourselves. When we contemplate the Christian life, we see ourselves as the heroes, struggling to meet divine expectations with human strength. We see ourselves as sincere, truehearted believers who try desperately to be faithful. Sometimes we seem to succeed. Other times we fail. But always we are earnest and valiant.

As a result of this natural, self-centered focus, we interpret the Christian life in a subjective way. Our attention is locked in to our own experience, good or bad. We think of our spiritual life in terms of our own feelings and interpret everything as to how it affects us as individuals. "What's in it for me?" we ask. We think of ourselves in the rather narrow dimensions of our own limited range of knowledge, ability, and experience.

One friend of mine became a Christian after a lifetime of living for himself. In a few weeks, the glow of his new life began to fade. Actually he had stretched the euphoria of his first encounter with Christ about as far as it would go. He had made little or no effort to maintain a close working relationship with his Lord. So he blew his stack one day, and the feeling was gone. He fell back on his same old self-image. "I'm not doubting Christ," he said. "But I'm not at all sure about myself."

For the person who thinks he is doing well and impressing God, this subjectivism leads to religious pride. For another it may lead to discouragement, because the Christian life is so difficult, and he seems to do such a poor job with it. Either way, the focus is on the individual and his courageous efforts to please God. All the while, he searches for that happiness he has been promised in the glowing testimony of the super-Christians he has heard.

Selfhood Beyond Self

Let me urge you now to think of yourself in a new way. As a Christian, your selfhood is focused in Jesus Christ.

The key to who you are is no longer within the bounds of your natural abilities, relationships, or background. Your identity transcends this time and place. Who you are goes beyond who your parents were and how well you've done up to now. You are now identified with One whose life cannot be contained in any period of time or any location or limited by any restrictions, even death. Your life is now inseparably intertwined with that of Jesus Christ.

Let me put it this way: Don't ever think of yourself without thinking of Christ. In fact, your major source of difficulty as a Christian may come at this very point. You often think of yourself apart from the status, strength, and resources of Christ. So let me say it again: Don't ever think of yourself without thinking of Christ. Once you identify yourself with Him, there can be no accurate definition of who you are apart from who He is.

Christianity is not a religion in which you give human worship to a legendary, long-dead prophet. (In fact, Christianity is not religion at all. It is a relationship that makes religion unnecessary.) Rather you become so united with the risen Christ that your life is intertwined with His, and He with yours. He is the center of all you are or ever will be. His presence is the force which shapes your character. You can never be separated from Him.

Did I hear you say, "That really sounds good"? Maybe you are thinking you'd like to feel that way about your relationship with Christ. You have wanted to be so close to God that He would never be far from your thoughts. But wait a minute. Let me make something clear. From God's viewpoint, you are already as much His child and as much united with Christ as you can ever be. When you put your faith in Him as your only hope of salvation, it's settled. You have begun the adventure of becoming.

You: From God's Viewpoint

How you feel about your relationship with Christ is not nearly as important as what God says about it. That's why I'm urging you to think about yourself in a new way. Think of yourself as God sees you in Christ. Don't let your old feelings block out the truth. The power to become means a new identity that is in terms of Christ rather than in terms of your own conclusions about yourself.

The key to your selfhood is in two New Testament phrases: "you in Christ" and "Christ in you." The first of these key phrases describes your standing as a child of God in Christ. The second describes your strength because Christ lives within you. Together they mean that you now have a new identity because of your identification with Christ. Paul said it well, ". . . it is no longer I who live, but it is Christ who lives in me" (Galatians 2:20).

Being in Christ means you are an insider as a child of God. The Father looks upon you as fully acceptable to Him in every way that Jesus is. Actually, only one man has ever been fully approved of God. That man was Jesus of Nazareth. In remaining perfectly obedient to the Father, He broke the hold of Satan on mankind. In dying in behalf of every man, He made a way of access to God. Now forgiveness of sins is possible for everyone who will rest his case on the price already paid at the Cross. Being in Christ means you participate in all Jesus accomplished for you.

The idea of your being in Christ is sometimes expressed

as "with Christ." Paul writes that the believer has died with Christ, was buried with Him, and raised with Him to new life. You also ascended with Him, to be seated in a position of honor at the throne of God. So you, too, are accepted and honored as one who sits with God. Since you have identified yourself with Christ in trusting Him as your Saviour, you have become a participant with Him in all He accomplished for you. In a sense, you were there when He died, was buried, and arose from death on your behalf.

In light of all these remarkable truths from the Bible, you can be no less than an entirely new person in Christ. As I already mentioned, "When anyone is joined to Christ, he is a new being; the old is gone, the new has come" (2 Corinthians 5:17). Never think of yourself without thinking of Him. You are in Him. He is in you. All He has gained is yours. All He experienced directly affects you today. It affects who you are and who you are becoming. In Him your own identity as an individual has significance far beyond the limited time and space of your present experience.

"That's Just the Way I Am"

In His death, you died. Being in Christ means you died with Him. When He died for sin, that sinful nature which enslaved you was taken to the grave. Jesus not only died for your sins to provide forgiveness; He also died for you, the sinner, to provide freedom from the bondage of sin. You, too, are dead to sin. You do not have to respond to sin's promptings. You can choose to reject the stirrings of your lower nature. Just as physical death frees us from the pain and weakness of this physical body, so your death with Christ frees you from the tyranny of your sinful nature.

How many times have you said, "That's just the way I am. I can't help it"? We usually say things like that when we're trying to excuse some bad habit or weakness. We feel victims of our own nature. We seem to be cursed with loose tongues, quick tempers, irritable reactions, negative attitudes, irreverent spirits, rebellious wills, and all sorts of dark moods and fears. But here's good news: You don't have to be like that anymore. You have died with Christ. There is no longer any necessity for you to put up with the ill-tempered expressions of the old nature.

In Christ you have new life because you are raised with Him. Just as your death and burial with Him means you are not bound by your own history and temperament, so your new life in Him means you have new possibilities beyond what you can imagine. An apparently successful friend in his forties responded to a description of Christian leadership this way: "I could never be like that. I just can't see myself ever being that kind of person."

We all tend to do that at one point or another. We draw an imaginary circle around ourselves and say, "This is the kind of person I am. These are my abilities and weaknesses. I can only become what my capacities and limitations will allow, and no more." But when you shift your focus from who you are in yourself to who you are in Christ, you remember that you are raised with Him to a new life. Now your abilities are of no particular consequence. Neither do your limitations set boundaries for your growth. The key is not who you are in yourself, but who Jesus Christ is. It is His life that is your new life.

The Bible also says you are seated with Him in the heavenly place. In other words, you are qualified in Him to take a seat in the presence of the King. You are perfectly acceptable with Him in Christ. Your acceptability does not depend on your performance, but on the fact that you are in Christ. His performance in your behalf includes you in the host of those who perfectly meet God's standards for approval. We will discuss this important area in greater detail in a later chapter.

Not only are you in Christ—identified with Him in His death, burial, resurrection, and ascension—but Christ is also in you. This means that your new identity is not an ideal you are left to strive for in the best way you can. Your new selfhood in Christ is assured as a reality by the very presence of Christ in your life. He is there to live that new life in His strength and character. That's why Paul wrote, "I have the strength to face all conditions by the power that Christ gives me" (Philippians 4:13).

Because you are in Christ, your natural self, with all your hang-ups, does not have to be your prison all your life. In Christ you died to that old self and with Christ in you you have the power to pull the sheet over every one of those old corpses, when they try to get back up. In Christ you are risen to a new life and with Christ in you the only One who ever lived that life is ready to live it through you this very moment. In Christ you qualify to sit in the presence of the Father, and with Christ in you that worthiness can be lived out day by day. *Hallelujah!*

Thinking It Through

• Several times in this chapter I have said it is *natural* to approach life in certain ways. By natural, I mean the way you would ordinarily think and act on your own. By now you see that your usual approach to life will not apply successfully to the challenge of being a growing Christian. In fact, being a Christian is not at all natural. It is *supernatural*. The Christian life will be fully impossible for you to act out in and of yourself. That is why you must learn to think of yourself in a new way.

• The key to this new way of thinking of yourself is this: Don't ever think of yourself without thinking of Christ. Since you have received Him as your Lord, there is actually no you outside of Him. Now that you are in Him, the old you who was outside of Him has died. All those natural things about the old you have been buried so that their grip on your future has been broken. You are now risen with Christ to a new life and a new future as a new you in Christ.

• So the most important thing about you now is not your name or your address, your hometown or your childhood, your web of human relationships or prestige in the world, your talents or your fears. Though all these factors are a part of who you are becoming, the most important fact about you that really tells who you are is this: You are in Christ and He in you. All the rest takes on new meaning when you see this as the key.

• This does not mean you have lost your individuality. On the contrary, you have only now found your individual worth and significance in Christ. Apart from Him, your whole world revolved around yourself, your plans, your pleasure. But now you are a child of God. All His promises are yours. Your life has meaning beyond this moment, because you are a child of the Resurrection, part of a new race of men in touch with eternity. Your life is inseparably united to the One whose heartbeat gives rhythm to the whole universe. "When anyone is joined to Christ, he is a new being; the old is gone, the new has come" (2 Corinthians 5:17).

The power to become is the power of a new way of thinking about yourself.

4

Getting Accustomed to Being a Son

When I was a boy, my parents could talk to me without saying a word. Just a frown, a raised eyebrow, a nod, or the slightest smile, and I knew what they were telling me. It's funny how children, even very small ones, learn to look toward Mommy or Daddy from time to time, to check out where they stand. It's like asking with a glance, "How am I doing?"

We never really outgrow that need for a sense of acceptance and encouragement. Every one of us likes to have somebody important to us say, "You're doing fine." Even when we're grown, some of us wish we still had a mommy or daddy to look up to from time to time and catch a glimpse of a facial expression that says, "You're doing okay" or "I don't think that's a good idea" or "Be careful" or "You're getting in over your head" or "Stop that at once!"

One of the greatest messages a child can read in a parent's face is, "I know you made a mistake, and you are embarrassed about it. But you are still mine. I love you. And everything's going to be okay." Unfortunately, though, some parents, and others—like big brothers, teachers, supervisors, husbands, wives—accept us only on the basis of our good behavior. When we do well, they like us and send us good messages, but when we get out of line with the rules, they cut us off.

There's a distinction we need to recognize. There's a big difference between saying, "I think you'd better change what you're doing," and, "I think you are stupid, and what you're doing proves it." Instead of getting the message that your behavior could use some improvement, sometimes you get the message that you are a hopeless case. Then it seems that no matter what you do or how hard you try, it's never good enough; and you stay frozen out because of your poor performance.

Seeing God's Face

What is God's attitude toward you? Have you ever wished you could see God's face and read just how He feels about you at the moment? Do you sometimes think of God as scowling at you and freezing you out? At other times, do you imagine that God is happy with you? In becoming the person God has in mind for you, it's very important that you know where you stand with Him.

Many Christians are never sure of God's attitude toward them. Even some who are sure they are God's children are not sure He likes them. After all, our performance is pretty inferior at times. God probably gets so disgusted that He wants to disown us. In fact, some people think He does just that: If you don't keep all the rules, He kicks you out of the Family. With a big angry frown, He says, "I've had it with you!"

Is that your idea of God's attitude? Does God like you or freeze you out, according to your performance? It's easy for us to think that way. After all, it seems that's the way people operate. And everybody knows you make it to heaven only if you keep God's rules well enough. Isn't that right? Listen to these words of the Apostle Paul: "But now God's way of putting people right with himself has been revealed. It has nothing to do with the Law . . . . God puts people right through their faith in Jesus Christ . . ." (Romans 3:21, 22).

Did you get that? God does not accept people on the basis of the Law—keeping the rules. God accepts people as right with Himself on the basis of their trust in Jesus Christ. Not only does God accept sinners as His children when they trust Jesus, He keeps on accepting them that way. God's attitude does not change as our performance changes. In fact, God isn't impressed with even our best behavior. He says all are sinners—period.

God's way of putting people right with Himself is based on the performance of Jesus Christ, not on our performance. Jesus lived a perfect life. Beyond that, He accepted the guilt for all the sins of every person and sacrificed His own life to remove that sin barrier. So Jesus' performance was perfectly acceptable to God. When we believe that what Jesus did was for us, then we are perfectly acceptable to God, too, even though our own performance is far below His standard.

How can you grow toward being the person God has in mind for you, if you think God doesn't like you and may kick you out of the Family any time? The answer to that is simple: You can't. If you are to have the power to become, you must have confidence that God is for you, and not against you. You must accept the fact that you are God's child on the basis of Jesus' performance and not your own. You must know that God loves you and accepts you, that His facial expression says, "You are mine. I love you. And everything's going to be okay."

God's Attitude Dramatized

The most beautiful New Testament story of God's love for His children is the parable of the Prodigal Son (Luke 15). You may remember this story. It's the one about the younger of two brothers, who asks his father for his share of the inheritance. The father gives each of the brothers his portion of the estate. Then the younger goes off to live a wild life in another country.

Eventually he runs out of money and friends and winds up on a pig farm, working for a foreigner. He is so hungry that he is just about to eat the pig slop. Then he remembers he is a son. He remembers he has a father who loves him. He remembers that even the servants at home fare better than he does in this pigpen.

He decides to go home. On the way he practices the speech he plans to give to his father, "Father . . . I have sinned against God and against you. I am no longer fit to be called your son; treat me as one of your hired workers."

When he gets home, he starts his speech, but his father interrupts when he sees that the son is really confessing his sins. He calls for a new robe for the son, a ring for his hand, and shoes for his feet. The father says that they are to have a big party and celebrate because his son was lost but now is found, was dead but now is alive. You may want to read the parable for yourself in Luke 15:11–32.

The Meaning of Sonship

The first truth we want to examine from the parable is the meaning of sonship. We are impressed that the young prodigal remembered he was a son. He remembered he had a father. The son, of course, represents you and me; the father represents our heavenly Father. One of the most serious mistakes a Christian can make is to forget or be unsure he is a son. There is little or no power to become, as long as you are doubting you are a son of your heavenly Father.

Throughout the parable—at home with the father, making selfish demands, in a far country, foolish living, losing everything, in the pigpen, returning home—the relationship did not change. The prodigal was a son. No matter what he did, he was a son. The father could have disowned him, but he didn't. So his sonship was based on the constant love and acceptance of the father, and not on the behavior of the son.

No matter where you are in the story of the Prodigal Son, your Father loves you and accepts you. If you are at home, in good fellowship with Him, He loves you and accepts you. If you selfishly demand your own way and are ungrateful for all His blessings, He loves you and accepts you still.

This does not mean He's not disappointed when you go astray, because He knows your behavior will ultimately bring you grief and will very likely turn out to be a detour in His purposes for you. But He knows, at the same time, that He can use your own foolishness to teach important lessons. So the Father loves you and accepts you, even when you behave like that.

If you are out in the far country, living it up, the Father loves you and accepts you. That doesn't mean He won't chasten you. The Bible tells us that when a father really loves his children, he disciplines them and punishes them. This actually proves his love for them and his acceptance of them. If they were not really his children, he wouldn't bother with them. But, because they are his, and he loves them, he goes to the trouble to correct them. That correction is not the kind of thing a child wants to experience, but later on he appreciates it.

If you are in the pigpen, out of friends, and out of funds, the Father's attitude is still loving acceptance. What a great truth this is. What a tremendous thought that God accepts and loves me, no matter what my performance. His love and acceptance of me are based on the accomplishment of Jesus in removing the barrier of sin and making it possible for me to be a son.

That is the meaning of sonship. I am a son of God because the Father Himself guarantees that relationship. He requires of me only that I believe it. He commands that I obey Him but wants that obedience to be a loving response of trust and surrender. When I demand my rights and leave for a far country of self-satisfaction, He lets me go. There are hard lessons to be learned, and He knows that when I return home I will be much wiser than when I left.

So what does this make me want to do, knowing that God loves and accepts me no matter how I behave? Does it make me want to go out and live like the devil? Does it make me want to be selfish and mean and unkind? After all, I know that no matter what I do God still loves me and accepts me and is prepared to forgive me. No, this great truth of sonship makes me want to thank Him, praise Him, and try to be faithful to please Him in every way. What love! What grace that God accepts me in Christ as a son, in spite of my sin!

The Becoming Gap

Let's understand the difference between *relationship* and *fellowship*. My relationship with God is that I am a son whom He loves and accepts forever. That does not change, because God maintains that relationship Himself. I did not earn the right to be a son. It is a gift from God. Since I didn't earn it, nothing I do will guarantee that I can keep my sonship. In the parable, the relationship, or position, the young prodigal had with the father never changed. He was a son throughout.

Fellowship, though, is the personal quality of the relationship, which at any given time affects the enjoyment of the benefits of that relationship. Did you get that? Well, in other words:

Relationship means who I am
  Fellowship means how I'm doing
Relationship speaks of my position with God as a son
  Fellowship speaks of my performance in light of God's will
Relationship does not change—I'm always a son
  Fellowship changes, depending on my trust and obedience

Relationship means that as a son I have all the benefits
     of sonship
Fellowship means that I can only enjoy these ben-
     efits when I trust my Father and obey Him

Though the relationship remained the same throughout
the prodigal's experience, the fellowship changed dramatically. Even though he was yet a son (relationship), he
wasn't getting along very well with his father (fellowship). Does that sound familiar? Sure it does! Every one of
us has been keenly aware, at times, that our attitudes,
words, or actions were not pleasing to the Father. We
have sensed the tension, the coldness, the loss of joy. But
who moved? Did God move away from us? No, we moved
away from Him, toward some "far country."

We have heard of the "generation gap," when people of
two different generations can't seem to get together. The
"becoming gap" is the space between our present stage of
maturity and the character and spirit God has in mind for
us. The becoming gap can be seen as the difference between our position and our performance. The goal of becoming is to close the gap so that you are, in practical
living, the person God says you are.

The becoming gap is also seen in the difference between relationship (as sons of God) and fellowship (a
matter of communication and harmony). I must stay close
to the Father, keep the lines of communication open, and
continually accept His will, if I am to make progress in
becoming who I am in Christ. God says I am His son, but
sometimes I don't think like a son or talk like a son or act
like a son of God. There's the challenge! There's the growing edge! In character, spirit, and behavior, God is seek-

ing to bring my performance into perfect harmony with my position as a son.

The prodigal demonstrated a real turn around in attitude, which made the difference in his fellowship with the father. At first his attitude is seen in the demand, "Give me what is mine." Toward the end of the drama, we see a totally different spirit, as he says, "Let me be like one of your hired servants." But, between these contrasting attitudes, the young man came to his senses. He saw things as they really were and said, "Father, I have sinned and am no longer fit to be called your son."

Applying for Second-Class Status

The confession of the prodigal is impressive in its sincerity and humility. He is repentant of his sin, sees the absurdity of his situation in light of the wealth of his father, and so goes home to admit his error and apply for a job as a hired hand. His speech goes like this: "Father, I have sinned against God and against you. I am no longer fit to be called your son; treat me as one of your hired workers."

Notice that he says he is "no longer fit to be called" a son. He does not say that he *is* no longer a son. He knows that his sonship is in the hands of a loving father. His membership in the family has not been revoked because of his foolishness and rebellion. But the reputation of the father may be questioned because of the son's behavior. He says he is not fit to be *called* a son. That has a familiar ring to it. Sons, but not fit to be sons. That is grace. God's salvation is only for sinners.

The prodigal makes a mistake, though. Since he thinks

he has forfeited his rights as a son, he applies for a job as a hired servant. Why does he do this? Maybe he feels that he should be punished for his sins, that he should be on probation for a while before being given the privilege of sonship again. This is a very human response. When we fail to be faithful to God, we feel guilty about it. So we apply for some kind of second-class status to salve our guilt.

The father, however, interrupts in the middle of his speech and calls for all the privileges of sonship to be restored immediately. There are to be no second-class sons in this house! What would this say of the father, if his own son were degraded to the position of a hired servant? No, the position of the son will not be downgraded because of his behavior. All the father wants to hear is genuine repentance and confession of his sins.

Have you ever thought of yourself as a second-class (or worse) Christian because of your poor behavior? Have you just accepted a position of inferiority, even though you confess your sins? Do you feel it necessary to mope around a few days or weeks because of your failure? Do you take it on yourself to run yourself down and punish yourself? If so, you are making a serious mistake. There are no second-class sons of God. You needn't apply for such a position. You may be a son out of fellowship or a son near to the Father's heart, but you are ever a son. Joyously accept your Father's forgiveness.

Getting Back What Was Lost

Even though there are no second-class sons, we can suffer serious loss when we break fellowship with the

Father. It is obvious that the young prodigal lost all the benefits and privileges of sonship when he left the estate of his father. That estate could well illustrate the territory of the will of God for a life. As long as we remain inside that area and maintain communication and harmony with the Father, we enjoy the benefits of sonship. When we leave for the "far country," however, we suffer loss. The losses come so gradually, at times, that we may not even notice until we are brought face-to-face with our stark poverty.

One of these benefits of sonship is access to the vast wealth of the Father. The young man took his share and left. In his hands, outside the father's rule, the money quickly ran out. When you and I begin to think of the resources in our hands as our own, we learn how limited they are. But when we stay within the protective rule of the Father, all He has is ours. The father's wealth was not diminished by the prodigal's foolishness. But as he demanded his own way, the young man soon found himself destitute.

A second benefit of sonship is symbolized by the robe which the son was given when he returned. The robe represented his acceptability, respect, and honor as a son of the household. In his journey to the far country, he lost the honor and self-respect which should characterize a son. His status was in question. When we fall into sin, we, too, lose the respect due a son of God. We, too, lose the dignity and self-respect of sons and begin to look like those who are not sons.

A third benefit which was restored to the son was symbolized by the ring for his hand. The ring was a signet bearing the official family seal. It allowed the son to act with the full authority and power of the family. He had lost his power to represent his father. So can we lose the power that comes only under the Father's authority. We can become spiritually weak and carnal. Only as we return to the Father's will do we find that spiritual dynamic restored.

A fourth benefit is symbolized by the shoes for the son's feet. Slaves did not wear shoes in that day. The son came home barefoot. He had fallen to the place of a mere slave. He had come into bondage because of his sin. In the far country he did not have the freedom which was supposed to be his as a son. He wound up in servitude to a foreigner, doing the most disgusting job a Jew could imagine: feeding pigs. When he came home, his freedom was restored.

So, inside the Father's "estate," the territory of His will and rule, we have the privileges of sonship. We have access to His vast resources. "Ask, and you will receive . . . ," He says (Matthew 7:7). We have the honor and respect which come with practical righteousness. "Be holy as I am holy," He says. We have the power of the indwelling Spirit for facing the challenges of life. ". . . when the Holy Spirit comes upon you, you will be filled with power . . . ," He says. (Acts 1:8). We have freedom from the control of the enemy. "If the Son sets you free, then you will be really free," He says (John 8:36).

Thinking It Through

Becoming the person God has in mind for you requires knowing where you stand with Him. Certainty of God's attitude frees you from many of the crippling misconceptions which keep Christians from growing. Determine now to build into the fabric of daily life truths we have noted in this chapter.

• A common error of Christians is that of confusing position and performance. As a child of God, your position is settled forever—with all its benefits. Your performance will not change God's acceptance of you as a son. Let me suggest that you read the parable of the Prodigal Son every day this week, in a different translation. Remind yourself of the truths we have noted. Begin your daily prayer time in thanksgiving for these facts, point by point.

• At times you may sense that your stubbornness and self-will have broken your special fellowship with the Father. But don't apply for a second-class status. There is none. God does not want us to spend longer feeling guilty than the time it takes to become aware of our sin and confess it to Him. Take a sheet of paper and catch up on your confession right now. Be honest with the Father, in a spirit of gratitude. Determine daily to be honest in such confession and keep the way clear for the warmth of unhindered fellowship with the Father.

• As a Christian, you can live in the awareness of God's constant and loving acceptance. But this awareness cannot fail to affect the way you relate to others. If the Father accepts us because we are sons, in spite of our performance, then should we not accept other Christians because they are brothers, in spite of whether or not their behavior pleases us? And what of unbelievers? Are they not those for whom Christ died? Stop and examine how you relate to friends, acquaintances, and strangers. Do you let their appearance and life-style restrict your acceptance and respect?

• Just as you rejoice in acceptance and love that do not

waver with your performance, so do others need these from you. Children, marriage partners, and friends will all respond to affection and respect that are not fickle and self-serving. If you really love someone, will you turn it on and off in an attempt to affect his behavior? Constant and dependable love will have much more influence than freezing-out tactics. Plan now for creative new ways to relate to loved ones on the basis of who they are, and not how they behave.

The power to become is the power of a sure standing with God.

5
Seeing the Bigger Picture

Walking up a path at a mountain conference center, my wife and I noticed two crows flying speedily by, overhead. A friend, meeting us on the path, commented, "Do you think she'll catch him?" I'm sure we looked perplexed for a moment. Then we realized he was talking about the crows. All we saw were two big, noisy, black birds. He saw a certain type of female crow chasing a male. He saw a dimension of reality about those birds we weren't equipped to see.

What we see around us depends on what we know. Two people can look at the same clouds and see entirely different figures in the shapes. Charlie Brown's friend saw famous paintings and historical figures, while he saw a horsie and a duckie. I look at a clear night sky and just see stars. My neighbor, who teaches astronomy, sees constellations and planets and calls many of the stars by name. That's because he knows a lot I don't know about stars.

What we look at is the same, but what we see depends on what we know.

This is the way it is with faith. How you see life and the world around you depends on what you know about it. If your knowledge is quite limited, you only see the obvious. But by faith you see a dimension of reality beyond mere sight, taste, hearing, smell, and touch. Faith is seeing reality in its full dimensions because we know something about God and His purpose.

We grow up learning how to read our surroundings by use of those five senses. "If you can see something, it's there. If you can't see anything, nothing is there." We learn to think like that. So seeing the dimension of reality only seen by faith doesn't come naturally to us. The sight of faith is an ability God alone can give us in the first place. Then how well we see by faith depends on how well we know God and His plans.

Normal sight gives us a three-dimensional picture of the world around us. We see things in terms of length, width, and depth. Only length and width can be seen in a photograph or painting. Artists try to give the illusion of depth in their work but it's only an illusion on a flat surface. Depth can only be seen with both eyes and adds that third dimension that gives the whole picture. I remember the realism and excitement of those three-dimensional movies that were once the fad. The picture seemed to come right out of the screen at us.

Seeing the full dimensions of reality by faith is something like being able to see more than just a flat picture of your world. You know there's more there than just the obvious aspects of life. God is at work, present in the affairs of men, carrying out His purpose for His creation.

By the sight of faith you see the depth of spiritual reality, as well.

The whole matter of becoming who you are in Christ is rooted in that dimension of reality beyond the natural world. It is basically a spiritual matter. So it's very important that you see the big picture of reality beyond the obvious. Paul explains that ". . . we fix our attention, not on things that are seen, but on things that are unseen. What can be seen lasts only for a time, but what cannot be seen lasts forever" (2 Corinthians 4:18).

So let's talk about faith. How do you get it? How does it work? Is it a *leap*, as we have so often heard? What's wrong when your faith is weak? Does faith mean refusing to use your reasoning? How important is faith, after all? First, let's look at a biblical definition of faith. Then I want to sketch five key steps in the function of faith.

A Definition of Faith

Sometimes we get the idea that faith is believing something, no matter how foolish it seems. Even if all the evidence seems to prove a belief is wrong, you hang on to it. That's faith. At least that's what some people seem to think. But we've already pointed out that there's more to reality than meets the eye. There's a whole world out there which you can't get hold of in an ordinary way. You can't weigh it, measure it, color it, or get your hands on it.

So we might naturally ask, "If there's no evidence for that other dimension of reality, how can you know it's there at all?" That's a good question: What is the evidence? Is there any evidence for the spiritual world, or does faith believe something is there even without any

evidence? That brings us to this well-known Bible definition of faith: "To have faith is to be sure of the things we
hope for, to be certain of the things we cannot see" (Hebrews 11:1).

The word translated "to be sure" was often used in
Greek to mean the basis for an agreement or business
transaction. It was a promise or contract. So faith means
we have a contract promising us the things we hope for.
What are these things we hope for? They are the things
included in the promises God has made to His children.
The Bible is a contract God has provided to spell out what
He promises to do for His children. Faith counts those
promises as good as done.

The second main word in our definition is translated
"to be certain." It was used in Greek to mean "proof" or
"conviction." *Proof* means there is enough evidence in a
certain direction to be confident about something. You
can have a conviction that it is real. We cannot see the
reality of the spiritual dimension, but faith sees the evidence needed to be certain of the things we cannot see.

Looking to See

Faith doesn't come naturally. You have to decide to
believe, to exercise faith. There always seems to be
enough evidence that God is *not* real: things go badly;
God is silent; He is unseen. At the same time, there is
always evidence enough to trust Him. What will you do?
It's like two people telling different sides of a story. Each
one gives his version, based on his own interpretation.

We need to consider all the evidence when we are deciding how things really are. If we look only at the obvi-

ous, we may miss the whole picture. Faith is a matter of deliberately looking at all the evidence and seeing God present and at work in even the most difficult situation. Faith is picturing what God plans to do on the basis of His promises and His record. Then faith has us act in keeping with the reality of that picture.

So faith is actually a special kind of sight. Some say faith is like "spiritual eyes." The Apostle Paul wrote that ". . . our life is a matter of faith, not of sight" (2 Corinthians 5:7). He is comparing faith with sight. Just as we need to see well to operate best in this material world, so we need to have spiritual sight to function in the spiritual dimension. We are used to the saying, "Seeing is believing." But for the spiritual dimension of reality beyond the five senses, we need to turn that around and say, "Believing is seeing."

How important is faith, from God's viewpoint? Is faith just an extra-spiritual quality which only super-Christians have? A good answer is in Hebrews 11:6: "No one can please God without faith, for whoever comes to God must have faith that God exists and rewards those who seek him." Faith is the only acceptable way to relate yourself to God. Trusting Him is the only approach that will result in His power and blessing in your life.

Since faith is so very important, let's look closely at how it works. I want to give you five key steps in the working of faith that will help you know how to live by faith. We will answer several important questions: How can I know if I have enough faith? How can I have stronger faith? What can I expect from God in response to my faith? Are there some special things to do in prayer that will insure an answer?

The Starting Point for Faith

Faith begins with God and His Word. Does that surprise you? Had I asked you where faith begins, you may have thought, "With me, in my heart." Sometimes we wish we had a spiritual dipstick, like the one we have for checking a car's oil, so that we could check the faith level in our hearts. But faith isn't centered "in here," within us; it is focused "out there," beyond ourselves. It isn't a substance or a virtue contained in our hearts, so much as looking away from ourselves to God.

Faith needs an object for its focus. You can't just believe generally. You must believe in something or somebody. Paul said faith is like sight. Our eyes are constantly trying to focus on some object. Even when things are rushing by us, our eyes keep trying to latch on to some specific thing to see. So it is with faith. Real faith requires some object for its attention. Christian faith focuses on God in Jesus Christ.

Sometimes we feel our faith is too weak. You have probably wished for greater faith at one time or another. But how does faith come? Paul writes, "So then, faith comes from hearing the message, and the message comes through preaching Christ" (Romans 10:17). Faith is ignited when the truth of God is presented to us. Not only is that true at conversion, but throughout our Christian experience. Faith increases as we gain new understanding of who God is and what He plans to do.

So I have faith, not in my faith, but in God and His faithfulness. The question is not whether you have strong enough faith to believe. Jesus said all that was needed was mustard-seed-sized faith. The question is not whether our faith is strong enough, but whether we are trusting a strong enough God. The more you know of the Word of God and His promises, the more your faith will grow. We are to ". . . keep our eyes fixed on Jesus, on whom our faith depends from beginning to end . . ." (Hebrews 12:2).

A Ray of Hope

The second step in the function of faith is this: The Holy Spirit causes hope to spring up in your heart as you hear the promises of God. We have already mentioned the importance of God's promises. In the definition of faith in Hebrews 11:1 faith is being sure of the things we hope for. These things hoped for are the thousands of personal promises in the Bible. One scholar says there are five thousand; another says seven thousand. Either way, God has given enough promises to kindle faith in us at every possible point of need.

When you see a truth in God's Word—either a direct promise or a fact about God—the Holy Spirit causes a personal sense of hope to spring up in your heart. God has said He will meet your needs at some particular point, and you say, "I hope that's true." Like a ray of light in the darkness of gloom and unbelief, the hope comes. Like a tender plant springing up in the parched ground of doubt and discouragement, hope springs up in your heart. You have a sense of expectancy and anticipation, as the Holy Spirit tells you God will surely be faithful to His promise.

This hope is not just wishing. Wishing has no substance to it, no foundation under it. It is like a vapor in the air: The first breeze of circumstance blows it away. But some people go on wishing: "I wish I could be a better person"; "I wish I didn't have this bad habit," and so forth. Hope, however, has a foundation under it. It has the authority and trustworthiness of God Himself and His promises.

You might say, "I wish I could decide which way to go." Then you read God's promise ". . . I will teach you the way you should go; I will instruct you and advise you" (Psalms 32:8). You say, "I hope that's true." The Holy Spirit gives you the assurance it is true. Then hope springs up in your heart; and you expect God to guide you, because He has promised. That expectation is the flame of faith, and God honors it.

Keeping Faith Alive

The third step in the function of faith is this: You must act on the promise of God, or the faith dies. Can faith actually die? Yes, it can. Faith is of such a nature that it must be expressed in some outward fashion, or it dies. We might say that faith needs a lot of fresh air and exercise to survive. If we do not act on the basis of our hope in some promise of God, that hope shrivels and dies. James writes that ". . . faith without actions is useless . . ." (James 2:20). This action may take different forms, depending on the promise. Many times it will be simply a matter of specifically asking God to meet the need.

"But why must we ask?" someone might say. "Doesn't the Bible say our heavenly Father already knows our needs?" Yes. Jesus did say that (Matthew 6:32). But Jesus also said, "Ask, and you will receive; seek, and you will find; knock, and the door will be opened to you"

(Matthew 7:7). Faith must be expressed outwardly. We must remember that the basis of the Christian life is relationship. Tapping the resources of God is not a mechanical matter. It involves a relationship between persons. We must open communication and enter into fellowship with our heavenly Father, in order to do the business of faith with Him.

"But doesn't God make His rain to fall on the just and the unjust alike? Doesn't the Bible say that?" Yes, it does (Matthew 5:45). And about all some Christians receive from the Father is rain. God desires to glorify His dear Son Jesus, through answering our prayers and taking action in our lives. If I refuse to trust Him on the basis of His promises, then Christ isn't praised because of my life. Others see no difference in what I receive as a Christian and what they receive as unbelievers. Remember, no one was ever converted, no matter how great his need, without opening communication with the living God.

What should you ask for? Well, some believers think God is too busy or not interested in the very personal things we might ask of Him. They feel that our prayers should be only for high and lofty "religious" needs like, "Lord, bless all the missionaries." No doubt God is interested in blessing the missionaries. But He is no less interested in the very personal needs I have. After all, He has counted the very hairs of my head (Matthew 10:30). When Jesus said *ask*, did He mean ask for material needs? When He said *seek*, did He mean seek direction? When He said *knock*, did He mean trust God for finding a way through obstacles in our path? If so, these are very personal needs.

I used to pray, asking God to *bless* a lot of things and people. But one day I asked myself, "What do you really mean 'bless this,' 'bless that'?" And I realized, "I'm not sure what I mean." I guess for me it meant, "Let everything be wonderful!" In Matthew 7, Jesus tells us six different ways that we are to bring our needs as requests to God. Then He says that if we, as sinners, know how to give good gifts to our children, how much more will our Father give good things to those who ask Him. *Good things* means specific answers to specific prayers to meet specific needs.

What should you ask for? I would say ask for what you want! (Are you thinking of asking for what you don't want?) If you ask for what you want, you are praying an honest prayer. What a shame only to pray, "Bless all the missionaries," when you have a very serious personal need you think isn't "religious" enough for God. Like Sears, God always reserves the right to substitute something of equal or better quality. And His catalog of promises spells out His preferences. He will be God. He will be sovereign. Even if His answer is not what you asked for, it will still meet the need much better than what you had in mind.

So often, as we pray, we put restrictions on ourselves that make us feel unqualified to pray. Shouldn't we pray only for the will of God, in the name of Jesus, and with clean hands and a pure heart? Yes, that would be very good. But if you wait until you feel perfectly qualified, you may never get serious about prayer. I have an idea that someone on his knees before God can learn a lot about the will of God and the name of Jesus and about clean hands and a pure heart. Go ahead. Ask your heavenly Father. He knows all about you and accepts you anyway, in Christ.

God Takes Action

The fourth step in the function of faith is this: God begins to answer when you begin to ask. God sets the processes in motion to bring about an answer to your request as soon as you begin to pray about it. In the tenth chapter of the Book of Daniel, we read a fascinating story of prayer. Daniel fasted and prayed for twenty-one days on the riverbank, until finally an angel of God arrived in answer to his prayer. The angel said he had been sent as soon as Daniel had begun to pray. He had been hindered for all this time by spiritual forces opposed to the will of God.

I'm not sure I understand all there is in this story. But I can see one thing clearly: God began to answer when Daniel began to ask. And so it is with us. When we begin to ask, God begins to work, perhaps behind the scenes and way out on the edges of our experience. Nevertheless, He sets things in motion to meet our needs. It may take a while, but we can be assured that God is working. Let's just be sure we don't give up. Like Daniel, let's be faithful and keep on praying until the answer comes.

The last step in the function of faith is this: We continue in prayer, with praise and thanksgiving, until God's answer is a reality in our experience. The Apostle Paul writes:

> Don't worry about anything, but in all your prayers ask God for what you need, always asking him with a thankful heart. And God's peace, which is far beyond human understanding, will keep your hearts and minds safe in union with Christ Jesus.
>
> Philippians 4:6, 7

Notice that we are to ask with a thankful heart, thanking God not only for what He has already done, but also for what He will do. Notice also that you are to ask God for what you need. Even though He knows our needs, we are to ask.

In the meantime, between the day we begin to pray and the day God's answer comes, what happens? We are kept by God's peace. We rest in the assurance that our Father will give us the best, as we trust Him. So His peace, which is far beyond human understanding, keeps our hearts from discouragement and our minds from confusion. What a wonderful promise!

Thinking It Through

• Two common errors are apparent today, concerning faith. One is the idea that faith is believing what you know isn't true. The other error is the idea that God has no choice but to do what believing Christians ask of Him. Both these approaches make the mistake of focusing faith on man, instead of on God. On the one hand, faith is like speculation—whatever I believe must be true, in spite of the evidence. On the other hand it is an attempt to manipulate God on the basis of my insistent belief.

• Let's remember, though, that faith is nothing more than confidence in God. It is accepting the fact of the supernatural dimension of reality because God has told you, in Scripture, what is there. Since this is true, the more you know from God about the unseen world, the better you see and understand it. True faith always depends on further information from God.

• Consider the idea that, in a sense, you accept everything you know by faith. It is so easy for us to be deceived. Many a magician or illusionist has made a career proving that. Things are not always what they appear to be. Our physical senses can play tricks on us. So, is it so strange that the biggest trick of all is that our senses are unable to perceive the spiritual dimension of reality?

• The truth which comes to us by God's revelation in the Bible shows reality in its full dimensions. Is it so strange that those who deny such a thing as the supernatural would not be able to accept the Bible? They already have their minds made up as to what can and what cannot be true. In their tight little man-made interpretation of the world, there can be no reality beyond the examination of the five senses. Theirs is a flat, one-dimensional concept of reality.

• When you see reality in its full dimensions, however, you are able to read what is going on around you. Your broader, wiser view is based on information an unbeliever refuses to accept. But remember that it is easy to slip back into that flat, one-dimensional outlook, if you do not maintain a balance of natural evidence and revelational evidence. And when there is an apparent conflict in evidence, you do well to believe God. We know He will not deceive us, though our senses sometimes do.

The power to become means seeing the full dimensions of reality.

6

Resolving the Inner Struggle

The story of Dr. Jekyll and Mr. Hyde, by Robert Louis Stevenson, is about the kindly physician, Dr. Jekyll, who finds a way to turn himself, from time to time, into the evil monster, Mr. Hyde. The various movie versions of the tale are filled with tension and suspense. We anxiously wonder when Dr. Jekyll will again turn into the shaggy-faced, fang-toothed monster.

Of course we all know it's just fiction. Don't we? After all, there could never be a man who had the nature of the kind and gentle Dr. Jekyll at one minute and, a few minutes later, had the evil and hideous heart of Mr. Hyde. Could there? Maybe this is why we like this story so well. Maybe all of us have found ourselves with two natures. At times we can be so kind and unselfish, generous and cooperative. At other times we feel mean and selfish, irritable and rebellious.

Can one person be both ways? You may as well admit it. Sometimes you don't feel like yourself. Part of the difficulty with having two natures is trying to tell which side of yourself is in charge. You may be doing very well—kind, gentle, helpful—and all at once you realize that you feel irritable, boastful, or unloving. It's so easy to be fooled into saying or doing something to let the cat out of the bag or, I should say, let the monster out of his cage!

We wonder how to get that ugly side of our nature under control. It seems as if there's a monster chained in the basement of our souls. Without warning, he shakes his chains and breaks loose, to come charging up the stairs and express himself some way. You say, "I wish I hadn't said that," or, "I wish I didn't feel that way," or, "I wish I didn't get so angry." We want to keep the monster chained up, but we're not sure how to do it.

One of the greatest Christians who ever lived had the same trouble. The Apostle Paul wrote, "I do not understand what I do; for I don't do what I would like to do, but instead I do what I hate" (Romans 7:15). Paul seems here to be saying the same thing we are, "Sometimes I don't feel like myself!" He had come to realize he was not always in perfect control of his own attitudes and responses. No matter how good his intentions, there was a sinful nature within which would express itself whenever it got the chance.

What a complex problem this is! Christians are supposed to be holy. So we hate to admit we sometimes have these dark, ugly feelings. We just try to keep ourselves under control, to perfect our act so we can play the part well when we need to.

Besides that, the whole thing is such a mystery. How do you talk about something you don't understand? And you feel bad enough about it already, without making a public issue of it! After all, someone might think you need psychiatric help if you admit to that inner struggle.

So what's the answer? If you are to make any progress at your becoming in Christ, you must solve the mystery of the monster in the basement of your soul. But here's good news. There are some very specific answers in the New Testament. One section tells how God has promised to solve this problem and what to do to take advantage of that promise. The verses I am talking about are the instructions of Paul in Galatians 5:16–23.

These instructions remind us again that there's not anything, no matter how subtle, no matter how personal and subjective, that God isn't prepared to deal with in our lives. I want to point out five things that are in these verses: a promise of God for overcoming our lower nature, an understanding of the problem in everyday terms, a principle to operate by which will keep the door shut on the monster, a profile of the two natures, and how to put the whole problem directly into God's hands. Are you ready?

A Promise to Claim

God provides us with a very encouraging promise: We do not *have* to satisfy the desires of our lower nature. Paul writes: "What I say is this: let the Spirit direct your lives, and you will not satisfy the desires of the human nature" (Galatians 5:16). Here the apostle acknowledges some important things. He admits there is a lower nature, with desires which should not be expressed. We have self-centered appetites that do not reflect the attitude of Jesus. Having these latent desires is not the problem—

expressing and satisfying them is.

How do we keep from satisfying these selfish desires? God's promise is this: Put yourself under the control of the Holy Spirit, and you will not satisfy the desires of your lower nature. This is a matter of putting the whole house under the authority of a stern Master who refuses to allow the monster free rein. He puts him in his place: out of sight and out of business.

God's solution is directly opposite to what we normally would think. The usual approach to the problem is, "I will not lose my temper today," or, "I will not be critical of others today," or, "I will not yell at the kids today." We tend to concentrate on the negative aspect of the problem, in an attempt to keep it under control. That reminds me of the man in the cough-medicine commercial who firmly declares, "I will not cough!" What he is actually doing is concentrating on coughing. So he coughs in spite of himself.

Psychologists have demonstrated that when we concentrate on a bad habit or a negative trait, we reinforce it rather than getting it under control. So God's remedy is just the opposite. He says we are to concentrate on the control and leadership of the Holy Spirit. Our attention is drawn away from the negative, self-centered side of our nature and focused instead on the positive character of Christ.

Early one morning I was jogging around the block. As the sun came up, I saw the long shadow of my own figure stretch out before me. Then I turned the corner, and the shadow fell away behind me. As long as I was running toward the sun, I was not even aware of the shadow. But whenever I turned away from the sun, that long, dark

figure ran every step with me. That's not a bad picture of
this promise of God. We are to ". . . keep our eyes fixed
on Jesus, on whom our faith depends from beginning to
end" (Hebrews 12:2).

Learning to Sort Fruit

A second key to winning in the inner struggle is given
in Galatians 5:17. Here Paul writes:

> For what our human nature wants is opposed to what the
> Spirit wants, and what the Spirit wants is opposed to what
> our human nature wants. These two are enemies, and this
> means that you cannot do what you want to do.

This gives us the nature of the problem we face in everyday living. The problem is twofold: There is a war going
on in you, and the outward result is up to you.

The two natures of a Christian are called by several
names in the New Testament. They are the *flesh* and the
spirit. They are the *old man* and the *new man*. They are
the *natural man* and the *spiritual man*. Whatever the
names, these two conflicting natures struggle for expression in every believer. Only by submitting to the control
of the Spirit of God can we see the struggle settled at any
particular time. Before this can be done, though, we need
to admit that there really is a struggle.

The second part of the problem has to do with my responsibility to decide about my own behavior. Paul says
clearly, ". . . this means that you cannot do what you
want to do." You cannot do everything you think of. You
cannot say everything that flashes across your mind. You
must monitor your thoughts, impressions, ideas, and re-

sponses, to decide which side of your nature has produced them. You are responsible for every word, attitude, and action! That's the practical form of this problem of the struggle within.

Have you ever watched fruit or nuts being sorted by hand on a conveyer belt? The workers sit along the belt and carefully watch as the fruit flows by. Their responsibility is to pull the bad pieces off the line and throw them away, letting the good fruit go on through for shipment. That's what we must be: fruit inspectors. We must examine every expression as the "fruit" of our responses flows by. We must throw out the unacceptable expressions of the lower nature and approve only the fruit of the Spirit.

There can be no doubt that Paul meant exactly that when he wrote these instructions:

> Sin must no longer rule in your mortal bodies, so that you obey the desires of your natural self. Nor must you surrender any part of yourselves to sin to be used for wicked purposes. Instead, give yourselves to God, as those who have been brought from death to life, and surrender your whole being to him to be used for righteous purposes.
> Romans 6:12, 13

Through what Jesus accomplished for us on the Cross, God has provided the power for these instructions to be carried out. We will look at that a little later in this chapter.

These two natures promote their ideas primarily through our thinking. Have you ever noticed how easily you can get started on a negative and self-centered, angry

and contentious train of thought? Once that kind of thinking gets cranked up, it seems to feed off its own mo-
mentum. Pretty soon you have yourself all worked up
about nothing.

What happens is that the devil gets you on this line of
thought and talks to you all day, without identifying himself. His suggestions seem to be your own ideas. After all,
you are the only one with access to your thoughts, aren't
you? No, Satan looks upon your mind as a suggestion
box. If he can get your attitudes and thoughts going his
way, he's pretty sure to foul you up.

If the enemy got you on the line and said, "Hello, this is
the devil speaking," you would hang up on him. But he
doesn't do that. He prefers to remain anonymous. As long
as the ideas which pop into your head are taken by you to
be your own thoughts, he knows he can fool you. But
when you start examining every idea that comes along,
you can measure them by the attitude of Jesus. Then you
are well on your way to resolving the struggle in favor of
God's desires for you.

A New Way of Deciding

So far we have said that God promises us that the sinful
nature will be kept under control if we put the Holy Spirit
in charge. Besides that there is a real battle going on in
each of us, and we are responsible for checking every idea
that would be expressed.

Now we face the question of how to decide which
thoughts, words, and actions should pass and which
should not. Our first solution might be to make a set of
rules to go by. In fact, there are already plenty of rules

around which we can use to decide what is okay and what is not. The next verse before us, however, gives us a different principle to decide by. Paul writes, "If the Spirit leads you, then you are not subject to the Law" (Galatians 5:18).

What does it mean to be subject to the Law? It means to operate on the principle of law. It means we decide in terms of good and bad, right and wrong. It means we are continually trying to measure ourselves by the standard of God's Law, as we understand it. We let the Law direct our behavior, attitudes, and thoughts.

The new principle, though, is this: When we submit to the authority of the Spirit and follow Him, we are not under the Law. The Holy Spirit will never lead us to disobey God, for He is God. But under this new principle for deciding, we are to be led by the Spirit directly. The Law becomes reference material for understanding the will of God. We do not go first to the rules to find out what we should do. We seek to follow the Spirit and let Him guide our interpretation of the rules.

On a plane to Baltimore one time, I began to talk with the man next to me about the joys of knowing Christ. He was very interested and open to the subject. He asked me if I was a minister. I told him I was. "I don't guess you drink, then," he said, fingering the cocktail glass on the tray before him. "No, I don't," I said, and changed the subject back to God's love in Christ.

He brought up the drinking again, and I could tell he was uneasy about it. "Your cocktail is not a problem to me, if it isn't to you," I said. The important thing at the moment was not my opinions on drinking, but this man's need to know Christ personally as Saviour and Lord. He relaxed, and our conversation continued toward a serious affirmation of faith on his part.

That was one of my better moments! Since I have personally seen drinking bring sorrow and tragedy to my own loved ones, I feel very strongly about it. It's wrong! But the Holy Spirit doesn't seem interested in promoting my opinions. When I follow His leadership, I do not push the rules—for myself or others.

The most important thing is an open and loving relationship with God and other people. My guide is not the Law of God but the Spirit of God, who makes the Law a warm and personal expression of God's will. In fact, the Spirit alone is the one who ". . . reveals the truth about God" (John 14:17).

When we let the Spirit lead, we won't have to be concerned about the rules. The commands and laws of God will fall into place. The Law can never make a person better; it only shows up how bad he is (Romans 8:3). The job of making us like Jesus must be done from the inside out. The Bible says that God sent Jesus ". . . so that the righteous demands of the Law might be fully satisfied in us who live according to the Spirit, and not according to human nature" (Romans 8:4).

Getting Better Acquainted

The fourth key to resolving the inner struggle is this: Get to know the traits of the two natures. In the next part of Paul's discussion, he gives two lists. One list tells what human nature does. The other list gives the fruit of the Spirit. Here are the two natures described:

What Human Nature Does *Galatians 5:19–21*	*What the Spirit Produces* *Galatians 5:22, 23*
immoral, filthy, and indecent actions	love
worship of idols	joy
witchcraft	peace
becoming enemies	patience
fighting	kindness
becoming jealous	goodness
becoming angry	faithfulness
being ambitious	humility
separating into parties and groups	self-control
becoming envious	
getting drunk	
having sexual orgies	

What a difference! These two kinds of character couldn't be more opposed to each other.

It is very important that we get to know these two natures as well as possible. Unless you know what to look for, how can you know what ideas and responses to throw out and which to keep? The lists above are only samples. There are many important insights in the Bible to help you decide what fits with the character and attitude of Jesus and what does not. In fact, this is where God's Law comes in. The instructions and commands in the Bible give us a detailed picture of the kind of life we will live when the Holy Spirit has His way.

A Funeral for the Monster

Listen to this last key truth for winning in the inner struggle: "And those who belong to Christ Jesus have put to death their human nature with all its passions and desires" (Galatians 5:24). Did you read that correctly? Did that verse say that the sinful nature, the old monster within, has been put to death? Yes, that's what it says.

In another place we read, "And we know that our old being has been put to death with Christ on his cross, in order that the power of the sinful self might be destroyed, so that we should no longer be the slaves of sin" (Romans 6:6). Yes, there's no doubt about it. Paul is actually saying that our sinful nature has been put to death in the death of Christ.

So the fifth key to the inner struggle is this: Agree to the position of death for the sinful self. We have already pointed out that position is not affected by how you feel. Position is assigned by God, according to His grace. Your position is sonship. You are a son of God. The position of your lower nature, the sinful self, is death. God says it is so. Do you feel it is so? You don't? Does that change the facts? No. Rather than adjusting God's truth to our feelings, let's adjust our feelings to fit God's truth.

Christians are well aware that Jesus died for their sins. But do you know that Jesus not only died to allow sins to be forgiven, He also died to allow the sinner to be set free? You see, I not only have the problem of what I have done, I have an equally serious problem with what I am. I am, by nature, a sinner. What is worse, I cannot get free from myself. So no matter if God forgives my sins, I am still bound to go on sinning. But when Jesus paid the price for sins, He also took the sinful nature of mankind to the grave. Now there is not only forgiveness for sins, but also freedom from sinfulness.

"Do you mean I should be perfect now?" That would be nice, but it's highly unlikely. You already know that forgiveness comes when you confess your sins (1 John 1:9). As with every other aspect of the Christian life, your faith is necessary. So it is with the death of the sinful nature and your freedom from its control. Your faith is necessary before this fact means anything in your life.

Just as you have forgiveness for sins only as you confess them, so do you have freedom from sinfulness only as you agree to the death of the sinful self. Paul writes that ". . . you are to think of yourselves as dead, so far as sin is concerned, but living in fellowship with God through Christ Jesus" (Romans 6:11).

The spiritual fact is that the old monster is dead. But to translate that spiritual fact into practical reality, I must exercise faith. Just as I confess my sins and thank God for His forgiveness, so do I need to confess my sinful nature and thank God that it has been crucified on Jesus' Cross. When I fall into slavery to my own sinfulness, I can stop and pray: "Thank You Father that my sinful nature died on the Cross. Thank You that I don't have to sin. I can say no and make it stick by Your power. At this very moment I can please You."

Do you see what this means? At any given moment, you can be free from the compelling impulse of your lower nature. As you continue to yield to the Holy Spirit, that moment can stretch into hours and days. So hold a faith funeral for the monster of sinful self—and good riddance.

Remember, though, that just as some tasty sins are hard

to confess, so can the sinful nature give you plenty of "good" reasons why you should yield to it. It's a simple question. Do you intend to do the will of God, or not? Your answer will determine whether you exercise the power to become, in Christ.

Thinking It Through

The problem considered here is that you sometimes don't feel like yourself. Even though you are a child of God, you find there is a struggle going on within, between your new Christian nature and your old sinful self. Let's consider some practical ways to exercise your power to become in this area.

• The key to winning in the inner struggle is refusing to become preoccupied with the monster side of your nature. Concentrate rather on the Christlike potential that is yours in your new nature as a Christian. A common mistake is the effort to correct all your faults instead of concentrating on growth in Christlike character. Think now of that quality you dislike most about yourself—like a critical attitude. Identify the positive quality that is its opposite—in this case an appreciative attitude. Now concentrate this week, not on controlling the negative, but on cultivating the positive.

• Begin today to be especially alert to what you say, what you do, how you relate to others. Can you see expressions of both natures in your behavior? Make a list of the traits you see in positive and negative columns. Now add additional positive traits you want to develop. Review this list every day, until you develop the habit of alertness to the two natures.

• A country song once declared, "Sometimes right's more wrong than wrong is." We tend to operate in terms of right versus wrong and good versus bad. But relationships are more important than regulations. Are you in the habit of pressing your personal preferences with the children, your mate, or co-workers? Think back over the past week and identify the times when your pushing your own idea of what is right strained relationships. Practice creatively emphasizing relationships over rule keeping. Chances are, the rules will be met much better.

• Notice that each of the keys to winning in the inner struggle is opposite in some way to our normal responses. Our tendency is to "do what comes naturally," to do or say what we feel like at the time. It's quite a discipline to learn to think first, to weigh the character of what you are about to say or do. But your power of choice is the greatest God-given power you have. You can be in control, if you choose to be. Today, practice exercising a firm, alert control over your responses, believing that God will enable you to make it stick.

• Attempt to extend the period of your self-control only to the present moment. Do not promise yourself you'll never lose your temper again. Only determine to respond positively right now. I do not mean you are to allow yourself the loss of control later. No, the point here is that the only real time you have is the present moment. As you determine to cultivate and express Christlike attitudes now, you can extend your control to ever-expanding periods. Only as you take charge now, can you make Christ Lord in your present moment.

• Being in the habit of responding in certain ways may make it seem unnatural to respond in new ways.

Nevertheless we do well to choose Christlike behavior, whether we feel comfortable with it or not. Carefully plan one positive gesture not now normal to yourself and act it out today. As you act in faith that God's way is best, you will find that your feelings about this new response will fall in line.

The power to become is the power to win the inner struggle.

7
Turning Temptation to Advantage

"I sure can't see any good in it," he said. "Just about the time I think I'm making real progress, something comes up, and I'm acting like my old self again. I mean, if it weren't for temptation, I could be a much better Christian. Why does God allow me to be tempted anyway? It looks as if He would want me to be more like Jesus. And I sure could be, if I didn't have all these problems."

The perplexity expressed by that young Christian is probably not at all uncommon. The more serious we become about growing in the character of Christ, the more we are made aware of the pressure of temptation. When we think of all the times we have compromised our high ideals and fallen into some sin, we wonder if we're making any progress.

Wouldn't it be better if God gave us some kind of immunity to temptation when we become Christians? Then, while everyone else is still in tune to the devil's enticements, we believers wouldn't even be bothered by them.

Then we would never fail. We would never sin. We could go on unhindered to become more and more like Jesus. Couldn't we?

We could go on in this line of thinking, to ask a lot of related questions. Why is there a devil anyway? Why did God make the world like this—with sin and evil and temptation and heartache? If God is all-powerful, couldn't He have made a world better suited to Christian living; or is God (as some theologians say) doing the best He can, but not quite able to get things in hand?

"I never even thought about all that," said another friend, as we were discussing temptation. "I never questioned the way God made the world, or whether He could have done a better job. After all, it's not God's fault. I'm the one who's weak and sinful and open to the pull of temptation. If I would just trust God and obey Him, there wouldn't be any problem."

There is some profit in such discussions as this. We are forced to think. We ponder weighty issues. But most of us find temptation and trouble problems at a more basic level than that. It's not nearly so much a philosophical issue, as it is a painful daily reminder that we have a way to go yet in our becoming. So let's look at the issue of temptation and what it has to do with our growth in the character and spirit of Jesus.

Learning Ruthless Realism

Some Christians say they can come to the place of living beyond the lure of temptation. They actually claim to live above sin and achieve "sinless perfection." Others say there is too much fuss over this prudish insistence on holiness. A little worldliness, they say, will allow you to be accepted and appreciated by non-Christians, so you can influence them. A vast number of others live in the smile-and-pretend territory between these two extremes. They just keep their sins neatly hidden away and hope nobody ever finds out about them.

Here's one truth we must get straight: We can only deal with a situation when we accept it honestly and realistically. As long as we try to ignore the reality of temptation and sin, we are in no position to do anything positive about it. So let's not spend our energy on discussions of "what if." Let's rather give our attention to learning why God has things running the way He does. Since God wants us to know the truth, He's always ready to make it known to those who are seeking it.

A good beginning point is to ask a different kind of question. Since temptation is a real problem for the Christian, there must be some purpose for it. Remember what the Bible says in Romans 8:28: "We know that in all things God works for good with those who love him, those whom he has called according to his purpose." That phrase "all things" covers everything. Even temptation would have to be included.

This is such an important idea that it must form the very foundation for all our thinking about how to cope with temptation. This verse actually says God works for good in all things. It is difficult to see how temptation could be a good thing, but we can know that in the midst of it God is working for good. And notice also that the key to all this is in the phrase "according to his purpose." There again is the grand design of the I AM.

Preparing for Battle

If we will accept as true the fact that God is working in temptation to accomplish His purpose with us, we can then move on to work out a plan for dealing with temptation. Life is filled with uncertainty. Sometimes it seems like a swamp of quicksand, bogs, snakes, and crocodiles. There's hardly a safe place to stand. Everywhere you step, there just could be danger.

Since we can't stand just anywhere, it's important to know where we're supposed to stand. The Bible tells us that God has brought us into His grace, where we now stand (Romans 5:2). What does this mean? God's grace is what He does for us which we could never do for ourselves. To *stand* is to be strong enough to win the battle. So we can win the battle of temptation if we stand on what God does for us which we could never do for ourselves. In other words, we stand firm in our confidence in Him.

We are like soldiers on sentry duty at a military outpost in a dark swamp. We are told to hold our position faithfully, if the enemy is to be overcome. That position is a firm confidence in God's strength. We refuse to budge from that station, because we know that we will not be safe anywhere else. Everywhere around us is the possibility of failure and defeat. "All other ground is sinking sand."

The whole military operation is in enemy territory, even though the rightful ruler is God Himself. We are issued a suit of armor to prepare for the conflict that is sure to come. We are told to "Put on all the armor that God gives you, so that you will be able to stand up against the Devil's evil tricks" (Ephesians 6:11). Listen to the rest of these instructions about the armor:

> So put on God's armor now! Then when the evil day comes, you will be able to resist the enemy's attacks; and after fighting to the end, you will still hold your ground.
>
> So stand ready, with truth as a belt tight around your waist, with righteousness as your breastplate, and as your shoes the readiness to announce the Good News of peace. At all times carry faith as a shield; for with it you will be able to put out all the burning arrows shot by the Evil One. And accept salvation as a helmet, and the word of God as the sword which the Spirit gives you. Do all this in prayer, asking for God's help.
>
> Ephesians 6:13–18

Hearing all that armor described reminds me of the boy David, when the king wanted him to wear his armor. He refused because it was too heavy and cumbersome. At first reading, the armor described in Ephesians sounds a little burdensome. But remember that all the things described here are automatically ours in Christ. And it's all designed to fit perfectly. In other words, we are to trust God about all these needed strengths.

Don Quixote rode around jousting with windmills, wearing a barber's shaving bowl for a helmet. But ours is a real battle. The battle is a spiritual one, and the armor is especially designed for that kind of conflict. Let's look over the list and note the significance of each piece of armor.

Belt of truth—refusing any pretense or hypocrisy
Breastplate of righteousness—sure of your rightness
    with God, through what Jesus has done about sin

Shoes of readiness to announce Good News—
everywhere you go being ready to share the Good
News of Christ

Shield of faith—your trust in God as your defense
against the doubt and lies the enemy throws at you

Helmet of salvation—your sure standing with God as
the crowning fact you trust against the enemy's
mortal blows

Sword of God's Word—the two-edged power of the
truth as your offensive weapon against the deceiver

Prayer—your constant communication with the
Commander-in-Chief who supplies all the resources for the battle

Remember that the purpose of this list of armor is not to
give you a set of duties or responsibilities as a Christian.
The purpose is to inform you about your equipment. All
of this is already yours in Christ. Your job is to put it on,
to believe God for these great truths of His power at work
in your life.

Developing a Strategy

As a sentry on duty in hostile territory, what are your
orders of the day? You hope to be able to deal with the
temptation the enemy is sure to throw at you. He is a
clever trickster and will stop at no deception or lie to trap
you and derail God's purpose in your life. At a crucial
point in the life of Jesus, He asked three of His closest
companions to wait with Him. When He returned, He
found them asleep, leaving Him to struggle with His
crisis alone.

". . . 'How is it that you three were not able to keep watch with me for even one hour?' " He said. Then He gave them instructions as to how to cope with the pressure of temptation. "Keep watch and pray that you will not fall into temptation. The spirit is willing, but the flesh is weak" (Matthew 26:40, 41). One familiar version of this verse says, "Watch and pray, that ye enter not into temptation . . ." (KJV).

Here is a two-fold plan for dealing with the problem of temptation. The first part is *watch*, remain actively alert for the enemy, vigilant for any move on his part. Peter, as a seasoned and mature Christian warrior, writes the same instructions, "Be alert, be on watch! Your enemy, the Devil, roams around like a roaring lion, looking for someone to devour" (1 Peter 5:8). The second part is *pray*, keeping the lines of communication open to Headquarters, ever ready to appeal for help. We have already noted Paul's encouragement to pray always.

The promise seems to be that if you will watch and pray, you will not enter into temptation. Now entering into temptation does not mean that you have lost the battle and fallen into sin. It rather means you are getting dangerously close, that you are losing your footing, just on the edge of the trap. There is that moment of uncertainty and hesitation when you aren't watching carefully and praying.

The Moving Parts of Temptation

Here's how temptation actually works: ". . . a person is tempted when he is drawn away and trapped by his own evil desire" (James 1:14). Notice the factors involved, as James describes them. First, there is the evil desire within you. The enemy knows he has no chance to influence you, except at some point of desire. And every one of us has the appetites of the lower nature, which might be stirred, if the right enticement came along. We have to admit, then, that the temptation actually is not only out there, but also in here. The appetite I have for some sin is the thing that makes temptation possible at all.

Look at the next factor mentioned. A person is tempted when he is drawn away. On the basis of the desire he already has, he can be pulled away from his proper position. He is drawn away from dependence on God and trust in Him. It is only as he begins to move away from this secure position that he enters into temptation.

Entering into temptation means you consider the suggestion of Satan as a live option, as a real possibility. It means you enter into a discussion with the tempter about the merits of the proposed temptation. This is what Eve did in the garden when the devil came to tempt her with the forbidden fruit. Without identifying himself, Satan got her involved in the discussion. (One of the funniest cartoons I've seen had Eve calling to Adam, "Hey Adam. Com'ere and look. A talking snake!")

Eve debated with the devil concerning whether God actually meant what He said about death as a penalty for eating the fruit. She believed his lie that God's real motive was to keep her and Adam from being wise and knowing what is good and what is bad. Then she considered how beautiful the tree was and how good its fruit would be to eat. She thought how wonderful it would be to become wise. Boy, did she ever enter into temptation! The devil surely doesn't need any help! But she got into a point-for-point sales pitch with him, and down she went.

This is exactly what Satan likes to do. He gets you on the line and talks to you all day without identifying himself. He gets you into the discussion, so you begin to think all these ideas are your own thinking. Pretty soon, with his sales pitch and your discussion, he's got you moving in his direction. This kind of entering into temptation can only be headed off when you watch and pray.

Anybody Really Hungry?

Notice, in Matthew 4:1–11, how Jesus handled temptation. He flatly refused to get involved at all. There was no dangerous moment of uncertainty and hesitation. After forty days and nights of fasting and prayer, Jesus was tired and hungry. The devil came to him and said, "If you are God's Son, order these stones to turn into bread." Jesus might have said, "I am hungry. There's no doubt about that. Do you realize how long I've been out here?"

Then the devil would probably have said, "I know what You mean. It just doesn't seem fair to me for You to have to go through all this. If I had something to eat, I'd sure share it with You. But go ahead, use Your divine powers to turn one of these stones into a nice, hot, fresh loaf of home-baked bread. What difference will it make? After all, if You've got the power, why not use it? You have to look out for Yourself, you know."

But Jesus refused to get involved in such a discussion. He was determined to do only what pleased the Father. So He answered the tempter in no uncertain terms: "The scripture says, 'Man cannot live on bread alone, but needs every word that God speaks.' " But the enemy didn't give

up that easily. He tried two more enticements, each designed to get Jesus to use His divine powers in a way the
Father had not intended. On the third attempt, Jesus said,
"Go away, Satan! . . ." and then quoted the Scripture
again.

The devil left Jesus at that point. There was no use
going on with it, since Jesus would not even begin to get
involved in the discussion. What Jesus did is exactly
what I think James meant when he wrote, "So then, submit yourselves to God. Resist the Devil, and he will run
away from you" (James 4:7). Jesus resisted him stead-
fastly. He would not budge an inch from His position of
trust in and obedience to the Father.

Making It Stick

The first half of the formula for resistance is submission
to God. Jesus' constant commitment was to please only
the Father. As we watch and pray, our prayer can be a
continual restatement of our surrender to the Father's
will. This surrender puts us under the Father's authority
and protection. We declare our resistance to temptation,
not in terms of our determination to be nice people, but in
terms of the very authority of God and His Word. As long
as the authority of God is established in our lives, the
enemy cannot get his own plans off the ground.

You may try the second part of the resistance formula
without the first, but it won't work. Both parts are necessary. First must come submission to God. Only then will
resistance to the enemy be effective. As we have noted, it
is an issue of authority. When one is in authority (God or
Satan), the other cannot be. So keep the Father in author-

ity, and you will be in a position to resist the devil with success. It will be in His authority that you do it, and not on your own.

What if a policeman knocked at the door and ordered, "Open up, in the name of Officer Schmelfungus!" Would you be impressed? Not likely. You might be amused and surprised, but you probably would not feel compelled to open the door. What a difference when you hear, "Police! Open up in the name of the law!" Behind that command is not just the influence of Officer Schmelfungus. Behind that command is the city, state, or federal government. It is the authority that counts.

When you are pressed hard by temptation, check out your authority. Is the Father in command? Are you deliberately under the authority of God? If not, you are attempting to resist the tempter alone, in your own strength. With that approach, you will surely lose, and the devil knows it. Remember that when you are under God's authority you can declare that authority which the enemy must recognize. He will have to leave you.

The Good of Temptation

We began this chapter with a question as to whether or not there can be any good in temptation. The whole process is undoubtedly a source of great distress and failure. What good can come of it? Well, James writes a rather surprising instruction that helps answer that question. "My brothers," he says, "consider yourselves fortunate when all kinds of trials come your way, for you know that when your faith succeeds in facing such trials, the result is the ability to endure" (James 1:2, 3).

Though the word *trials* is used in this Bible version, the original word is the same as the one translated "temptation." Any trial or trouble is a source of temptation, as we are tempted to fail to trust God with it. At the same time, any temptation is a trial. That's the very point James is making. These trials are tests of your faith. Whenever temptation comes, the real issue is faith. In the midst of the pressure, will you trust God or not?

Notice the rather surprising comment by James that we are to consider ourselves fortunate when all kinds of temptations and troubles come. Why? Because these very testings can result in growth. We can become more and more steadfast. Our faith can be strengthened. All the devil's attacks are aimed at some point in our confidence in God. That's why, as we noted earlier, our shield is faith.

A television commercial for Volkswagen showed the kind of testing done on the VW Beetle to prove its quality. One of those little cars was shown attached to a shaking machine that bounced it up and down mercilessly. While it was bouncing, there were other machines attached to the doors and hood to open them and slam them shut over and over. Why would a manufacturer put one of its cars through all that? Are they trying to destroy it? No! They are trying to identify weaknesses so that they can be strengthened.

Temptation can have the same result in our lives, if we see it in the right perspective. Instead of a dreaded source of trouble and failure, temptation can actually be turned to advantage. You can consider yourself fortunate in the face of such testings, because you know you will experience a joy and growth that would not be yours apart from the temptation. In fact, there could be little growth in Christian character if there were no trouble and temptation.

Cleaning Dirty Windows

Would you expect Satan to tempt you where you are strong? No! Then where would your crafty enemy be most likely to attack? Right! He'll hit where you are weak. He will look for a weak point in your armor, an area of immaturity, a point where you are not trusting the resources of the Father. His aim is to get you sidetracked, if only temporarily, from the purpose of God for your life; he tries to get you, even unknowingly, to reject the authority of God and choose to suit yourself.

One part of our strategy is to watch for the enemy. We must remain alert to his approach, or we will find ourselves going astray before we realize it. (He prefers it that way.) But as you watch, keep on watching. Notice the precise point at which the temptation comes. Could you safely assume that this is a weak point? Is the enemy actually doing you the service of pointing out a chink in your armor, a weakness in your character?

Every one of us suffers from blindness to our own faults, to some degree. It's really hard to be objective about your own areas of need for growth in Christlike character and spirit. But we cannot strengthen a needed area of growth unless we see it. Neither can we trust God to work in us for becoming, when we aren't even aware of those specific areas of immaturity. But God is ready to use the temptations of the enemy to signal us about our weaknesses. It is those very areas He desires to strengthen.

Watch closely. What do you see? Do you fall again and again to some temptation in the area of irritation and anger? Could it be that the Father wants to show you just how self-centered and demanding you are? You are angry and irritable because people and events don't go to suit you. Is it possible you are still insisting on having things your way rather than trusting God for His will to be done, even in the little things?

Are you tempted at the point of some impure and destructive habit? Does the Father want to point out to you that your body is the very temple of God? Does He want you to see that you are not your own, but are bought with the price of the Cross? Does He want you to see that your own willpower is not the key to discipline? If it were, you could boast about it. Perhaps He wants you to give up and trust Him with that habit. He will succeed where you have failed to conquer it.

Does the enemy press you about material things? Are you sometimes consumed with envy and desire? Do you find yourself falling for the same old lure every time? Is there always some new purchase that will be sure to make you happy? Could it be that the Father wants you to see that you are really not trusting Him with what He has put in your hands, that you have made the gift more important than the Giver? Does He desire to show you the abundance of His riches, when He can trust you to handle them as He wishes?

Watch closely. Notice those areas where the pressure comes. Sometimes they are so very subtle. Search God's Word for His answer. Ask the Holy Spirit to show you the real weakness behind surface appearances. Then, at each point, you can be sure that the resources of the Father are fully adequate to meet the need. Never forget that He is working in you, right now, to form the character of Christ.

Our lives are like windows. The light of the presence of Christ can shine through to light the darkness around us. But if the panes are dirty, the light can be dimmed, and even blocked out. Every point of pressure we feel in temptation is aimed at some dirty window, some weakness in our character. If we know that God works in all things, we know He can point out to us where the light of Christ is not showing. As we trust His forgiveness and grace, we can clean those dirty panes.

Thinking It Through

• Most Christians think of temptation as a necessary evil, something to put up with here on earth, that we'll be rid of in heaven. But let's realize that any aspect of life, no matter how distressing, can be used by the Father to our good. Once we settle that in our thinking, we can deal more creatively with anything that comes along.

• Give a little thought now to those points where you suffer the most persistent temptation. Sometimes the obvious weakness we see obscures the real issue. For instance, one man found that his distressing preoccupation with women was really connected with his failure to be a responsible and loving husband.

• There is really no point in our becoming when we arrive. The character of Christ is fathomless. There are always new, more subtle areas for growth. There is no time when we can safely stop watching and praying.

• Remember that what Jesus accomplished for you on the Cross not only covers your sins, it also covers the sinner. As you become aware of an area that goes deeper than mere deeds, take that to the Cross, too. That inner character of the sinful nature is also covered. Never forget that as a new creation in Christ you don't have to be like that anymore!

The power to become is the power to turn temptation to advantage.

8
Overcoming Your Energy Crisis

The energy crisis continues to be in the news. The experts tell us there's a shortage of oil and natural gas. Utility bills continue to go up. New forms of energy are still in the testing stages. I recently read an article describing what life would be like if we actually ran out of energy. Cars would be parked, rusting, in the streets—with no fuel to run them. Electric lights would burn only dimly, and then on a strictly reduced schedule. For a society used to all the power we need, when we need it, that's a frightening picture.

As we continue our study of the power to become, the question may begin to nag you, "How can I do any better than I've been doing? After all, I surely have tried!" And I'm sure you have. Any serious Christian has a familiar pattern in his efforts to please God. There seems to be a cycle: enthusiasm—cooling off—apathy—dissatisfaction—enthusiasm. We give it all we've got for a while. Then, like a tired runner, we sit down and pant awhile, completely exhausted. We're victims of an energy short-age already!

Finding the Right Kind of Power

There's no doubt about it. Living the Christian life takes energy—and lots of it. But what kind of power is it? Does it take willpower to follow Christ? Jesus certainly put an emphasis on choosing and deciding. What about intellectual power? It's not easy to understand the deep truths of God we need to grasp if we are to make progress in our discipleship. What about emotional power? The love, joy, peace, and patience we must have do not come easily. Some faithful, church-going Christians would add that physical power is also needed!

We used to live near Lake Whitney, where electric power was produced as the water rushed through the dam and turned giant generators. What power! That water literally thundered through the openings. I was impressed. But it would have been foolish had I taken a bucket of that water home and poured it over the electric motor in our air conditioner. That's the wrong kind of power! Let's not forget that the Christian life is a supernatural life. It cannot be lived in any kind of natural human energy. We not only need a lot of power to become like Jesus, we need the right kind of power.

You are familiar with two kinds of electric energy. You know, there's the battery kind and the plug-in kind. Actually, the kind of electricity which comes from the power company is AC, or alternating current. This means the current is constantly changing directions. The other kind of electricity is called DC, direct current. The current flows steadily in one direction with DC, what we think of as battery electricity. These two kinds of current will not power the same machinery without going through a converter.

Our energy problems in living the Christian life are not unlike the distinction between AC and DC. The kind of power we need is spiritual power. The kind of power we have is natural power. We are used to operating throughout life on the basis of our own natural energies. We can think. We can decide. We can feel. And we can take physical action. But unfortunately (or fortunately), none of these is the kind of power needed in knowing God personally and accomplishing His purpose.

Spiritual power is the kind of power which can only come to us through the "converter" of our faith. Jesus said, "But when the Holy Spirit comes upon you, you will be filled with power . . ." (Acts 1:8). That was the spiritual power needed before those early Christians could boldly be His witnesses, even to the ends of the earth. As they waited in prayer, they were trusting that God would supply the power needed for this superhuman task. And He did!

When the power of the Spirit filled them, these disciples were "charged" for their task in every way: emotionally, volitionally, intellectually, and physically. But their new powers went far beyond their old natural abilities. They were obviously new men in their boldness, persuasion, confidence in God, and faithfulness. What was fully impossible to them before, was now no problem.

What a temptation it is, though, to try to live the Christian life in the energy we use to do everything else. Instead of trusting Him, we operate on the basis of trying harder. The harder we try, the more obvious it becomes that we just can't be the person God calls us to be. Then you can either give up, just perfect your act and pretend, or rest awhile and try, try again. Either way you are facing mission impossible, with no hope of success. So let me recommend that you give up on that approach and adopt a plan for depending on God's power.

A Working Relationship

One of the mysteries in living by the power of God is the problem of how my own natural abilities and God's supernatural power mix in the everyday situation. We have heard the formula, "Work as if it all depends on you; pray as if all depends on God." That is excellent advice. But it still doesn't explain how I can operate in the power of God without depending on my own abilities.

Jesus makes a statement that helps a lot in answering this question. He says, "I am the vine, and you are the branches. Whoever remains in me, and I in him, will bear much fruit; for you can do nothing without me" (John 15:5). Just as the branch must remain in the vine, so we must remain fully dependent upon Christ, if we are to bear fruit. All the resource for fruit bearing is in the Vine and the branches only get it by drawing on the Vine.

The most difficult part of the statement is when Jesus says, ". . . for you can do nothing without me." Even as we hear that, we know very well we can do some things without Him. We can even do some good things without Him. But we suspect that what we do without Him amounts to nothing. What we really need to know is how to do something in His strength, and not in ours.

What a staggering thought! God, the Creator of the universe, has determined to do His work through frail and sinful creatures such as we. Paul writes in praise "To him who by means of his power working in us is able to do so much more than we can ever ask for, or even think of" (Ephesians 3:20). God intends to accomplish things beyond our imagination, through the exercise of His power in us.

Our working relationship with God is neither all God nor all us. Even though all the spiritual power comes from God, He does not exercise that power, except through the faithfulness of believers. Paul was called by God to take the Gospel to every person possible. And he was dedicated to that superhuman task. "To get this done," he wrote, "I toil and struggle. . . ." Hold it! That's certainly a try-harder approach, if I ever heard one! But wait. Let him finish. ". . . I toil and struggle, using the mighty strength which Christ supplies and which is at work in me" (Colossians 1:29).

That's the way it works. We are to give it all we've got. But we work hard, not because it all depends on our efforts, but because we know God is at work with the mighty strength of Christ in us. I work to obey God, because He is working, not because He is not. I study God's Word, not because I don't have a teacher, but because He is teaching me. I share a witness of Christ, not because people are turning away from the Gospel, but because God is drawing them to Himself. I see Him at work every time I launch out with confidence in Him.

A Lifetime Project

God's work in our lives is not just a random turning of the gears. His purpose is clear. "Those whom God had already chosen he also set apart to become like his Son . . ." (Romans 8:29). This is what we have called becoming who you are. This process of becoming is the continuing work of *salvation*, the Bible's term for all God wants to accomplish in your life. Some important instructions at this point are found in these words of Paul:

> . . . Keep on working with fear and trembling to complete your salvation, because God is always at work in you to make you willing and able to obey his own purpose.

> Philippians 2:12, 13

Again we see the working relationship. You keep on working because God is always at work. Notice the writer did not say we are to work occasionally. Rather we are to keep on working. Sometimes we may become tired and discouraged, even wanting to give up. But God never gets tired. He never quits. "So let us not become tired of doing good; for if we do not give up, the time will come when we will reap the harvest" (Galatians 6:9).

We are to work at the project "with fear and trembling." Our Christian discipleship is not to be a hobby or a source of entertainment. It is serious business.

A young artist had the unusual privilege of working for a brief time with a master painter. The young man was so earnest to take full advantage of the time. He arranged his small studio in perfect order before the famous artist arrived. He was careful to pay close attention to every comment, to listen much and talk little, and to give the master painter full rein to do whatever he wished during the brief lesson. Our attitude toward the Christian life should be this attentive.

The Bible says we are God's masterpieces (Ephesians 2:10). At the same time, we are given a part of the responsibility for how the project turns out. I can think of at least three reasons why we should approach such a task with fear and trembling. First, think of the importance of the work. God is actually building the very character of Christ into us. Then, think of who you are working with: the Creator of all that is! ("I'm working on this project with a Friend." "Is that right? Who are you working with?" "God.") The third reason for fear and trembling is that it would be just like us to ruin it!

Like a master sculptor, God chips off a little here, smooths out a rough place there, and steadily continues to mold my character and spirit into the likeness of Jesus. A news report told of a man who is planning to carve a giant statue of Sitting Bull, in the side of a mountain, with a bulldozer. The reporter asked, "Do you really think Sitting Bull is in that mountain?" I'm sure it may seem unbelievable at times to think that in you and me God really intends to carve out the character of Jesus.

Specifically, God is working to make you willing and able to obey His own purpose. As we cooperate in this project, God works on our desires. He is seeking to transform our "want to" so that our desires will fit in with His purpose. As new creations in Christ, we have new desires. But the old desires are also with us. God is working to give us a longing to be obedient to His will. Besides that, He is at work to give us the ability to do His will. How can we lose in an arrangement like that?

Power and Authority

Sometimes we are not sure about the difference between power and authority. We may even use the two
terms to mean the same thing. Actually, though, authority
means the right to rule, while power means the ability to
get things done. If you have authority, you have been
given the official right to make decisions and tell others
what to do. If you have power, you have the ability to do
something. We have discussed the power to become who
you are. But what does that have to do with authority?

In the world, power comes before authority and estab-
lishes authority. We see this every time some revolutionary leader takes over a government by force. Because he
has the men and guns, he forces his way into the right to
rule. In this country the power is in votes rather than
guns, but power still brings authority. With God's power,
things work just the opposite. Instead of power getting
authority, authority brings power. God only shows His
power where His authority is established.

This is very important for us in desiring God's power in
our lives. God does not work in power where there is no
one trusting Him. He has decided to do His mighty work
only in the lives of people who have trusted and ac-
knowledged Him as Lord. Jesus had the power in His life
to do mighty things. But He said He only did what the
Father authorized Him to do. The miracles He did were
evidence that He was surrendered to the authority of the
Father. So Jesus operated on the basis of the authority He
had from God, and the power came. Finally He said, "I
have been given all authority . . ." (Matthew 28:18).

So, as Christians, we do not need to fret over the problem of power. All we need to do is pay attention to the

matter of authority. As long as we surrender fully to the authority of God in our lives, His authority will be established there. When God's authority is established in us, His power will always be present for whatever He wants to do. Like a good soldier, we are not to worry about whether we will be given all we need to fight the war. All we are to do is obey our Commander and trust Him for all the resources.

When I was fourteen, I was somehow made senior patrol leader of my Boy Scout troop. I was not at all strong enough to make the big boys in the troop pay attention to my leadership. But I didn't worry about the necessary power to get the job done. All I knew was that I had been given the authority to be the leader. So I exercised my authority with all the boldness I could muster. Amazingly enough, the rest of the boys honored my leadership. (I had also made the biggest, meanest boy Sergeant at Arms, to maintain order.)

So it is with you and me in our desperate need for the spiritual power necessary for God's will to be done in our lives. All we have to do is make sure the unquestioned authority of God is established through our surrender and obedience. When God is in charge, He will provide all the power necessary to do what needs to be done. Again, as at every point in the Christian life, the key is our own trust in the Father and yielding to His will.

Thinking It Through

• Have you suffered from an energy crisis in your efforts to be a faithful Christian? What have been the results? When we operate in our natural energy, the outcome is predictable: a rather bland, do-it-yourself version of the Christian life. But the supernatural energy of God produces an altogether different result. Just imagine what God wants to do in your life!

• Do you find it hard to trust in the kind of power needed for the Christian life, rather than your natural abilities? Let's admit it. It *is* hard. Maybe we should say it's just not natural. Operating in spiritual power will have to be a deliberate choice. It will become more normal only as you continue to choose to depend on God's power at work in you. But don't ever think you have it down so well that you don't have to consciously choose.

• If God is actually at work in your life, what is He doing these days? How would you explain your part and God's part in the work God wants done in and through you? Remember that your side of the partnership could well be summed up in the words of the hymn by John A. Sammis, "Trust and obey—For there's no other way To be happy in Jesus, But to trust and obey."

• The point of focus in your special energy needs for Christian living is this: Concentrate, not on power, but on authority. Let your attention be on remaining consciously under the authority of Christ. As pockets of resistance are cleared up, His authority will be increasinly established in every facet of your life. With the establishment of that authority comes His power to do what He wants done. So when you become aware of your natural weakness, check whether all the territory of your life is consciously under the command of Christ. The issue is authority. The result is power.

The power to become means all the energy for becoming is yours.

9
Tying It All Together

We'd spread all the pieces out on the dining table and leave the puzzle there for several days, until it was finished. Every member of the family could be seen, from time to time, leaning thoughtfully over the unfinished picture, trying to find the only proper place for another piece. On the puzzle box was a picture of what it would look like when we finished. By matching colors and shapes, we could eventually arrange all those interlocking pieces to form an exact copy of that picture.

Putting a puzzle together is an almost impossible task without a pattern to follow. As long as you have that picture of the finished project before you, you know what you're doing. But so many of us approach the Christian life with misconceptions of one sort or another. So we struggle and fret and sometimes throw up our hands in frustration. We're never quite sure how it all fits together.

In these chapters we have spread out some of the key pieces for making sense of the Christian life. Some important parts may yet be missing. But you can find those, too, if you're serious about putting it all together. You may also have picked up some pieces of "truth" through the years that just do not fit anymore. There are some rather common ideas that have no place in the picture we have sketched here.

We have by no means addressed every problem we might face. In fact, we have dealt only with the rather narrow subject of your own very personal struggle for growth in Christ. There is much more to the Christian life. But to a large extent we are never quite able to make much "pilgrim's progress" until we first begin to understand the pilgrim. So let's take another look at the ideas we have discussed and relate them to the broader dimensions of the Christian life.

The Question of Becoming

The current emphasis on identity and personhood is not at all out of order as an approach to the Christian life. Jesus' key question was, "Whom do men say that I am?" But since none of us has arrived, a more appropriate question for us might be, "Who are you *becoming*?" In your very being are the seeds of becoming. You were created for a purpose. Until you get sight of that purpose, you will never know who you are.

The natural restlessness we feel about this becoming finds us making many empty attempts at happiness and fulfillment. We tend to see life in terms of achievement and accomplishment rather than growth. As a result, many men devote their entire lives to doing and building what only dies either with them or soon afterward. Who we are and what we are about can only be seen properly in terms of the timeless dimensions of character and spirit, of relationship and growth.

So we will not aim for accomplishment, but for growth. Behavior comes naturally from the kind of person you are, revealing the character and spirit within. Being comes before doing. God wants to build into us the very character of Jesus Christ. With that will come the kind of doing which reflects that character. At the same time, we will not wait until arriving at some kind of perfection before we behave in a way characteristic of our ideal. We act in the faith that God is at work, even now, to form His character in us.

Our aim, then, is not to do something, but to become somebody. Flowing from that becoming will be the kind of doing centered in God's grand design for us. It is the kind of doing not possible without the becoming. In my character goals, I aim at growth, not some kind of flawless perfection. I close the gap between who I am in God's sight and whom I see myself now to be, not by concentrating on my failures, but by keeping my eyes on Christ.

Where to Begin

I've always enjoyed the story about the farmer attempting to give directions to a stranger who had lost his way. After several attempts, he gave up in frustration and said, "Mister, you can't get there from here!" Well, there are some places to start in the Christian life that will not get you where you want to go. Jesus pointed to the only place to begin, when He said, "You must be born again."

The problem of a right start is not related to our good

intentions, our circumstances, or our behavior. The new beginning is needed deep within the heart of who we are. In all creation we see that the nature of a creature predicts his outlook and behavior. So it is with us. We are made in the image of God. But a malfunction in our character has turned us from focusing on our Creator to focusing on ourselves.

Nevertheless, God refused to give up on us. He provided a way for a transformation of character to begin within us. This new birth is the birth of a new nature within, through the very presence of God in our lives. Through the Cross of Jesus Christ, the sin barrier has been removed. Now the beginning of a new relationship with God is possible. His grand design for us is such that this spiritual rebirth is the only effective beginning for our becoming.

So the problem is not out there, with my circumstances and situation. The problem is in here, with who I am. As I face up to that fact and accept responsibility for my choices, I can choose to get in step with what God wants to do in my life. As a new person in Christ, I see a whole new factor introduced into my situation. That new factor is a new me. And every day brings new possibilities for growth.

Your Self-Concept

Psychologists tell us that your own self-image forms a circle of possibilities around you, which limits and defines who you are and what you can do. Such a self-concept develops through the years, as we take note of our failures and successes, what other people think of us, and what our fears tell us. In our approach to the Christian life, we bring all this baggage with us. What we see ourselves to be becomes a role we inevitably play.

As a Christian, though, the center of your world shifts from self to Christ. You now define who you are in terms of the new person you are in Christ. You see your possibilities in terms of the vast potential of His abilities. Your identification with Christ in His death, burial, and resurrection for you means you have a new future. You are not bound to your old nature. You don't have to be like that anymore. The new key to who you are and who you are becoming is Jesus Christ.

Never think of yourself without thinking of Christ. In a sense there is no *you* apart from *Him*. Christianity is just that radical an identification with the living Christ. The life God has in mind for you is fully impossible for you in and of yourself. But in Christ the unlimited possibilities of divine purpose are open to you. Your life has meaning beyond this moment because you are part of a new race of men who are in touch with eternity.

So write a new definition of who you are. Look closely every time you are tempted to say, "That's just the way I am." Stop and acknowledge that you don't have to live within those narrow limits anymore. Your life is inseparably united with the life of Him whose heartbeat gives rhythm to the whole universe. You can live beyond yourself in Him. Your future is wide open in the grand design of God for you.

Understanding God's Attitude

Have you ever wished you could see God's face and know just how He feels about you at the moment? It is easy to tie His attitude toward you to your performance.

Since people usually accept and respect us on the basis of our performance, it is natural to assume God operates the same way. Since your record is spotty at best, you could well come to the conclusion God is considering having you expelled from the Family.

Our acceptance with God, though, is not based on our performance. It is rather based on the performance of Jesus Christ in our behalf. No one "makes it" with God by doing something that will impress Him. He accepts us only as we trust what Jesus has accomplished for us. It is on that basis—our confidence in what Christ has already done—that we are accepted as sons of God. And that same approach applies throughout our becoming.

It is important to see the difference between position and performance. Your position as a Christian is sonship. You are awarded this privilege through the work of Christ on your behalf. Sonship can never be improved, nor can it ever be lost. It is maintained by the grace of God. Your *performance* should never be designed to impress God and make points with Him. How you behave is rather an expression of praise and gratitude as a son.

Another way to put it is to contrast the ideas of relationship and fellowship. Your relationship with God as a son is established by His grace, as you trust Him. You cannot earn it, nor can you improve on it. Fellowship, on the other hand, is a matter of personal communication and harmony with God. Your choices are a determining factor in the quality of your fellowship with the Father. Your trust and obedience at this point makes all the difference.

There are certain privileges of sonship which you only enjoy as you remain in fellowship with the Father. We saw that illustrated in the parable of the Prodigal Son. Sometimes we're tempted to punish ourselves when our performance has been poor and fellowship is strained. But remember that the Father is always ready to forgive and restore us. The only requirement is that we be honest about our sins and accept His forgiveness. There is no place for second-class sonship. You are either a son in fellowship or a son out of fellowship, but always you are a son.

The Mystery of Faith

You can't see what you don't know is there. We just naturally do not see the dimension of reality beyond the five senses. It's another world altogether, but nonetheless real. As Christians, however, we must operate not only in the natural dimension, but in the supernatural as well. We must see the full dimensions of reality—but that's not easy, because you can't see what you don't know is there.

So faith begins with God and His Word. The truth about what is out there in the spiritual dimension can come to us only from out there. Speculation by man as to what is beyond his natural senses always leads to creative and highly imaginative error. Revelation, on the other hand, means that God has made Himself known to us. He has revealed Himself in the person of Jesus Christ and the written Word—Scripture.

God is at work in the world and in your own life. But you are not likely to see what He is doing, unless you know what He has said He plans to do. As you learn of God and His purpose in the Bible, you begin to see the unseen. You begin to be able to read what is going on in the full dimensions of reality. You are not limited to the natural realm. You can live by faith.

Faith means you involve yourself in the goings on of that unseen dimension. You act on the basis of who God is and what He has promised to do. You see things happen in response to that faith, as natural circumstances and events are dramatically affected by unseen movement in another dimension. You are simply choosing to operate in terms of the truth from beyond. The evidence is there for the reality of God, and you choose to act on it. As you deliberately learn more and more of God's revelation in Scripture, your faith increases, because you only see what you know is there.

The Struggle Within

An area of growth that challenges us as much as any is the inner struggle between the two kinds of persons we can be. On the one hand is the self-centered nature of the *natural man*. The other alternative is the Christ-centered nature of the *spiritual man*. The Bible says there is a battle raging between these two natures, for expression in our thoughts, words, and actions. It is up to us to decide which side will dominate.

The most common approach to this challenge is to attempt to repress the self-centered, hurtful nature. But by concentrating on overcoming my bad habits, I focus on the negative and actually strengthen them. The scriptural instruction is just the opposite. Paul writes that we are to give attention to the control of the Spirit and thus edge out and overcome the lower nature. Again, we must remember that our aim is not to eliminate all our faults, but to grow in Christlike character.

So the promise is given that if we will concentrate on submission to the control and enabling of the Holy Spirit, we will not give room for the expressions of the sinful self. We can learn to monitor our own thoughts, attitudes, and behavior. Thus we can allow the expression of the kinds of qualities consistent with the character of Christ. We are not out of control. We do not have to act as we feel and say what we think. By deliberately yielding to the Spirit of God, we trust His control.

Our behavior is not shaped in terms of good and bad or right and wrong. Attitude and spirit are more important than our opinions about the rules. God's Law is given warmth and life by the direction and leadership of the Holy Spirit. Obedience to the Spirit will inevitably take the form of behavior pleasing to the Father and in keeping with His Law. Legalistic rule keeping, however, often violates the very heart of God's commands.

Coping With Temptation

If there's a fly in the ointment for the Christian life, it must be temptation. Appetites within and enticements without make an almost unbeatable combination. Again and again, we find ourselves falling into some trap that hinders our progress in God's purpose. So we try to stay away from temptation (that's not a bad idea), and steel ourselves for a willpower battle that will surely come. All in all, it's a bad situation only to be resolved in heaven.

There is a positive approach, however. Since the Bible says God is at work in all things to accomplish His purpose in our lives, we know He can even do something positive with temptation. But let's not fail to be realistic. Sin is a serious problem which is counterproductive to the purpose of God. Temptation, though, is not sin. It is but a prelude to sin. We can handle temptation with the wisdom of faith, and we can learn from it.

We know that the enemy is most likely to attack at some point of weakness. As we watch and pray, we refuse to get into any discussion as to the merits of a proposed enticement. But we also watch to see the precise point at which the temptation comes. We know that at that very point we can find a need for growth in the character of Christ. So the enemy has actually done us a favor, providing we don't fall for his line, in pointing out a specific opportunity for becoming.

God could have made a different kind of world, one without sin and evil, without Satan and temptation. But He didn't. So we do well to concentrate our efforts at understanding the world He did make. Though it appears to be unfriendly to the Christian life, this world is actually a proving ground for Christlike character. Apart from tests of our faith, we would see little growth, if any. Again, the Father does all things well.

Preventing a Power Failure

A high-energy concoction that was really supposed to rev up her motor was recommended to one of my friends. The trouble was that the stuff tasted so bad that she couldn't bring herself to drink it. No doubt many of us have wished for an infusion of energy for the Christian life. The Bible obviously promises such power. But there seems to be a mystery as to how to plug in to it. So most of us just try to tackle the challenge of Christian living with the same kind of energy we use for everything else.

What we need, though, is a different kind of power. Our volitional, emotional, intellectual, and physical powers just won't get the job done. The Christian life is supernatural, and supernatural power is needed. It is a spiritual endeavor calling for spiritual energy. This is just the kind of power God wants to supply for every need. It only comes, however, as we trust Him to do in us and through us what we could never do on our own.

The key to this spiritual energy is in the matter of authority. God does not work where He is not trusted to work. Only as we submit to His authority, will He exercise His rule. Unless He is in control in our lives, He is not going to be at work there. So where the authority of God can be established through our surrender, His power can be demonstrated. Any lack of power, then, is a problem of authority.

What an amazing thing to ponder. The Creator of all that is chooses to work in my life to accomplish His purposes. He actually takes me, with all my questionable qualifications, as a partner in the fulfillment of His grand design. But again, all the power is His. But the choices are mine. Will I deliberately choose to get in step with His will? The possibilities are beyond my imagination. What an opportunity!

Thinking It Through

• Over and over we have pointed out that the natural approach to these questions is usually the wrong approach. At every point, we face the same contrast. There is the world's way and the way of the Father. Thinking in terms of God's approach to life is not normal to us. But it can be. We can program our thoughts with the truth of the biblical outlook. We can choose to adopt a new way of thinking and, as a result, come to a new way of living.

• As I have said, this whole book has been devoted to the challenge of our very personal struggles with the Christian life. But God has much more in store for us than just learning to cope with our personal difficulties. His purpose goes far beyond the individual victories we may experience. He is at work to bring all of creation into consistency with Himself. And you, yes, you, are privileged to have a part in that.

• The one power God has given you by which you can actually overrule Him is your power of decision. You can choose your own destiny. God has granted you that freedom. But, at the same time, He holds you accountable for your choices. What you decide to do with today, with this present moment, will affect all your tomorrows. Choose boldly. Be disciplined in your decisions. You are walking with the One who holds heaven and earth in His hands.

"But as many as received Him, to them gave he the power to become . . . ."